PRAISE

COMPASS LINES

"Messick writes about the wilds of the world—from his first cabin in Fairbanks to traveling in the Everglades, South Korea, Syria, then back to Alaska—but all with an eye for the search for self-understanding, if not the quest for why we live in the first place. This is a writer who can summon up a caribou hunt, a fight against a forest fire, or the trapping of a lynx, with vivid detail and moral complexity. An authentic, compassionate, and most of all honest voice about the real last frontier."

—LEIGH NEWMAN, author of *Nobody Gets Out Alive*

"In this mix of memoir, travel, and nature writing, Messick eschews the bravado of the adventure tale, and instead invites us into the introspective root of his own restlessness, ultimately finding the home and connection he seeks in Alaska. Messick's stories are beautifully told—whether relating his travels in Damascus and Antarctica, canoeing the swamps of Florida, or working on fire crews throughout the Southwest and Alaska, Messick is a skilled storyteller. But it's his self-reflection and humility that gives this book such depth and wisdom. A pleasure to read!"

—DARYL FARMER, author of *Where We Land* and *Bicycling Beyond the Divide*

"Essayist John Messick's indelible evocations of travel and its delicious paradoxes carry the reader nomadically across the globe before home, in a luminously drawn Alaska, is realized. Messick is the kind of person who vacations in Mongolia—it's true!—but nothing smacks of escapism in this moving collection; here, venturing out affords the narrator an opportunity to examine, with a rueful self-scrutiny, his inner life, rituals worth preserving, and the nature of love and companionship, to name just a few. This memorable journey brims with an earned wisdom that often borders on befuddlement, which, after all, may be its own form of wisdom."

—CHRIS DOMBROWSKI, author of *The River You Touch: Making a Life on Moving Water*

"*Compass Lines* is a morally engaged journey into the wild places of the world and the wild places of the heart. I enjoyed exploring, alongside John Messick, all the vividly-described places in this book: the borderlands, the Northwoods, the Florida glades, the fire lines of the far west, neutrino-rich Antarctica. And I was grateful for how seriously he takes his responsibilities as a parent, a writer, and a citizen of the earth."

—DAN KOIS, author of *Vintage Contemporaries*
and *How To Be A Family*

"*Compass Lines* is at once a wild globe-trotting adventure, love story, and a beautifully introspective journey revealing the importance of our human connection with nature—all tied together with heart-strings and a good old fashioned Alaska-style blue tarp and some duct tape. The masterful storytelling and sage-like wisdom makes for one helluva compelling read. Easily one of my favorite collections in years."

—DON REARDEN, author of *The Raven's Gift*

"My wife and I read *Compass Lines* aloud and savored it daily: the outrageous adventures, the deep honesty, the light touches of humor and so much more. It made us laugh and cry and stare at each other in wonder. Mostly though, it enriched us and inspired meaningful conversation, as the best books often do. At one point John Messick reflects on 'how a place that seemed so close to the far edge of the world could make me feel so centered.' Maybe because some lines are circles, and the journey never ends."

—KIM HEACOX, author of *The Only Kayak*
and *Rhythm of the Wild*

COMPASS LINES

JOURNEYS TOWARD HOME

JOHN MESSICK

PORPHYRY
PRESS

MCCARTHY, ALASKA

© 2023 by John Messick

"For the Children" 12-line excerpt as epigraph. By Gary Snyder, from
TURTLE ISLAND, copyright ©1974 by Gary Snyder. Reprinted by
permission of New Directions Publishing Corp.

Book design by Katrina Noble.
Composed in Adobe Caslon Pro and Sweet Sans Pro
Cover art by Kristin Link.
Author photo by Jeremy Pataky.

Printed and bound in Canada on 100% post-consumer recycled paper.

All rights reserved. Except for brief quotations in critical articles or
reviews, no part of this publication may be reproduced or transmitted in
any form or by any means, electronic or mechanical, including photocopy,
recording, or any information storage or retrieval system, without permission in writing from the publisher. ∞

Published 2023 by Porphyry Press
Post Office Box MXY
McCarthy 22B
Glennallen, Alaska 99588
https://porphyry.press/

LIBRARY OF CONGRESS CATALOGING-IN-PUBLICATION DATA ON FILE
Library of Congress Control Number: 2022951881

ISBN 978-1-7367558-3-9 (paperback)
ISBN 978-1-7367558-4-6 (e-pub)

For Mollie,
and for Matthew & Helen

CONTENTS

Refrigerators at the
End of the Road

IN 2010 I drove up the Alaska Highway to Fairbanks with a woman I wanted to marry. The cabin we moved into had no running water. Wires dangled from the ceiling. At night squirrels chewed through the insulation in the roof, and when the temperature dropped that first fall, the walls leeched so much heat I needed a car scraper to see out the windows.

The yard was full of broken stuff. Fifty-gallon oil drums, a broken fridge, old fencing, tires, lumber, unidentifiable metal parts. Two cars sat on blocks in the driveway.

I learned the back roads around town. Almost every gravel cul-de-sac contained household appliances that local kids had dumped for target practice—dryers, fridges, washing machines, televisions, and rusted hunks of highway equipment. Late-night gunfire quickly became a signal somebody had dropped off another metal husk to shoot up.

The girlfriend I moved up with stayed a full month before we broke up. We'd been dating for almost three years, and this was the first time we'd lived together. Until Alaska, our relationship had been patched together between globe-trotting adventures—

Antarctica, Oregon, Namibia, Australia—calling each other on satellite phones, tacking out emails, scrawling love notes on birch bark.

I had pitched the move to Alaska as a way to merge our itinerant lifestyles and settle down. I knew moving in together would mean a steep learning curve, and I knew my eccentricities—fidgeting, hyperactivity, and brashness—could be tough to live with, but I really believed in us, and I was certain she did too. So when she left, I assumed it was due at least in part to the sketchy neighborhood, the shifting piles of industrial trash, and the lack of an indoor toilet in our cabin. I believed she simply wanted to live somewhere warmer, somewhere closer to her family, somewhere that didn't include me. Even though she'd left no room for any delusions that we might reconcile, I still hoped maybe she was just homesick. When she left, I was heartbroken.

I moved to a different cabin farther from town and found stuff in the yard there too. Previous tenants had left behind a rusting woodstove. I discovered moose bones, rotted firewood, more abandoned cars, a snare drum.

At first I tried to clean everything up. I inventoried. Organized. Then one day, hauling a load of tires to the transfer station, a guy pulled up beside me and asked if he could have them. They were bald, cracked, and about ten sizes too small for his pickup. I began to suspect that the stuff in my yard and the bullet-riddled scrap heaps along the dead-end roads might be a kind of cultural artifact I didn't yet understand.

I started paying attention to people's garbage, and once I looked, I found abandonment everywhere. Canoeing past the ghost town of Franklin in the Fortymile River country on a fall moose hunt, I came across a crane someone had driven down the frozen river decades ago, the giant tracks and arm rusting back into the permafrost. Fighting a wildfire in a forgotten corner of Fort Wainwright one summer, our crew unearthed bandoliers of live ammunition. The bullets dated back to World War II. A friend's father kept a stack of closet doors he had bought at an auction under a blue tarp behind their house. They'd been there for twenty years, slowly being reclaimed by alder, willow, and spruce.

I've heard people argue that this collective hoarding instinct so common in the Far North is a holdover from territory days, when homesteaders sometimes waited years for replacement supplies. I don't buy it. In Fairbanks, and in the house on the Kenai Peninsula where I now live, all the amenities are nearby: Walmart, Home Depot, Safeway, curbside trash pick-up, even appliance disposal programs sponsored by the borough. And yet, when we moved to our place on the Kenai, the yard was strewn with the rusted pieces of a dump truck.

I know this stuff is junk—appliances dumped by some wanton guy who doesn't give a shit. But I think this garbage is also a pathological response, indicative of our refusal to let go. Maybe we're scared that throwing away our old trash will deprive us of some essential and abstracted freedom. Maybe this garbage is the mark of a frontier mentality, where exploitation and abandonment are the status quo. Or maybe we keep these things around because we feel afraid, and we need to believe in a net that will keep us safe.

←——————→

I grew up among dairy farmers and deer hunters in rural northwest Wisconsin, and I struggled to fit in as a kid. I was fidgety and bookish; where I lived, those were character flaws. I left home for college, and after graduation I left the country.

Overseas, feeling like an outcast seemed an essential virtue. I grew to love the anonymity of foreign cities, the strangeness of unfamiliar roads, the smell of new foods, the sight of odd landscapes. I saw nomadic living as a moral imperative. I traveled from country to country, collecting knickknacks and stories, convinced I understood places because I experienced them with fresh eyes and because I wrote in journals along the way. I dumped the souvenirs and full notebooks into an old trunk at my parents' house each time I returned home. Years passed. The trunk filled with T-shirts, cheap tribal pendants, ugly paintings, stacks of brochures, train tickets, empty booze bottles, and rambling notebooks—the accumulation of an idealized version of myself. The only thing missing, I believed, was someone to share it with.

A couple months after my girlfriend left Alaska, I learned that she had moved to a town in western North Dakota, a place—if anything—lonelier, windier, and colder than Alaska. The breakup, I realized, was my fault. I had been so self-assured we were compatible, so desperate for us to work, I never noticed her veiled resentments or the slow distance she put between us. I had applied the same ideas to our relationship that I applied to the rest of my life: I believed movement could force a happy ending. My obsession had paralyzed her.

Discovering that my philosophical outlook on aimless travel had ruined my relationship was a revelation. Alone in my little cabin surrounded by broken-down appliances, I sought out new kinds of intimacy, and I found it in unexpected places. I gathered and froze berries that first fall. The next summer, I caught and canned my own salmon, hunted for caribou. In winter, I stood on the porch at fifty below, watched my breath shimmer, and felt in the silence the same rush I had felt in the jungles of Central America or in cities across the Middle East. I realized that in those faraway places, I experienced the same doubts, sought the same answers, told the same stories of loss and love I told myself while trying to be still.

I started going to church again, to an onion-domed cabin on the outskirts of town, listening to the Russian Orthodox liturgies I'd been raised with. At the paschal service in spring, during the procession around the church building at midnight, the sky shattered in a display of aurora—shimmering green and purple northern lights danced through the atmosphere.

"Christ is risen!" cried the priest. The parishioners answered, "Indeed, he is risen!"

In that moment of mystery and light, the swirl of green waves in the subarctic sky threaded together with my growing love of this place, and I realized that here, more than anywhere I'd ever visited or lived, I felt connected.

The difference between aimless wandering and a journey to family and community can be difficult to discern, but I must illuminate the paths I traversed, for they have led me from wanderlust to wild horizons. Thomas Merton wrote of a desert monk named Agatho, who "for three years . . . carried a stone in his mouth until he learned to be silent." I wonder: what must I do to listen to myself?

The broken machinery in my yard is part of my journey. It may seem incongruous to dream of both distant lands and local garden plots, but we tend to forget, too often, that everything is connected. The scrap heap in the brush creates a boundary between the familiar world and the wilderness, and the abandoned refrigerator serves as a fulcrum between contradictory ideas—rooted and roaming, nostalgia and expectation. It symbolizes for me the search for balance that has led from the lonely life of a drifter to the joys I share with my wife and children.

←———→

Two weeks after I finished college, I moved to South Korea to teach English. I was twenty-one, and I still wonder why I took the job. Korea is high on the list of most densely populated places, and crowds overwhelm me—I once had a panic attack in Costco because the lines were too long. In Korea every street corner had an Internet café, business dinners were part of my job description, and the mobs of people were inescapable.

So when I couldn't cope with the madness, I took a vacation to Mongolia. I flew out of Seoul and a few hours later landed in Ulan Bator.

The jeep I rode in from the airport smelled like mutton. A herd of goats bleated and crossed the road. From the hill overlooking the city, I would have never guessed that a million people lived in the valley below. There were no lights. I could see stars overhead. I hadn't seen a star in three months. Ulan Bator seemed practical and rough as sandpaper. Despite the Soviet-bloc-style apartments and government buildings, the city felt almost transient.

The next day I took a minibus packed with more people than seats to the town of Kharkhorin. The original highway had long since crumbled away, and we bounced across the steppe on a derelict road. I leaned out the open door for a better view. Nothing broke the horizon but a few sand dunes and a peppering of horses.

Always there were horses. Mongolians have perfected the art of horsemanship. Mongolian horses are tiny things, smaller than most ponies, but tough enough to ride for days across the Gobi.

I ate horse jerky and horse stew. In the rural areas, people offered bowls of yellowish fermented mare's milk called airak. A Russian man I met, who had spent a month in the country, said,

"These Mongols, my friend, they even screw on horses. I know. A woman taught me."

I'm not much of a horse person, but I wanted to see the countryside. In Kharkhorin I rented a bed in a *ger* pitched behind a coffee shop, and I paid the store owner to rent a horse for a week. Even coffee shop owners kept horses.

The owner's cousin arrived that afternoon with my rental horse—a mangy gelding whose ribs rippled along his sides. I saddled him with what looked to me more like an assortment of rags and wood blocks than a saddle. When I climbed on, my feet nearly reached the ground. But we rode the hills for nearly a week, and that horse never faltered, never balked at my amateur handling; he could gallop flat out for a kilometer without getting winded.

I didn't know where to go or what I was doing, so I enlisted Chuluun, the owner's cousin, as a guide. Several of the coffee shop owner's horses had gone missing a few valleys over, and I was informed that I would help Chuluun in the search. Chuluun was my age, and he smiled with his gums. Most of his teeth were rotten.

For three days we rode along scree slopes and across windswept valleys where yak, goats, and horses had grazed the steppe into a lawn. We stopped to visit *gers*—round, movable houses insulated with wool—known elsewhere as yurts. Families fed us fresh yak butter (quite tasty), curdled yak yogurt (not as good), and dried yak cheese (tasted like sandstone and ammonia). I drank homemade vodka and almost fell off my horse.

Occasionally, other men joined us in our search, which after a while didn't seem like much of a search at all. Once we skirted our horses around a Buddhist shrine, fluttering with prayer flags, and when I wasn't skilled enough to navigate my horse around the shrine, the men waited for me to show the proper respect. We descended to a fenced-in spring, where we dismounted, and after several shots of vodka, a few sniffs of snuff, and a pipe passed around the circle, Chuluun smacked my horse abruptly on the hind flank. He reared up on his tether and tore the fence apart. The men fell over laughing while I spent ten minutes chasing the horse across the steppe. He calmed when I caught him, and together Chuluun and I repaired the logs on the fence.

We stopped one afternoon at the ger of a man named Baldaarch. His wife offered us airak. I had come to like the sour, boozy flavor of the drink.

We sat in silence for several minutes. Neither Chuluun nor Baldaarch spoke English; we communicated through pantomime. Then Baldaarch crawled under the bed and pulled out a car battery. He brought me outside with him, around the edge of the *ger*, and fiddled with the connections on a satellite dish mounted to the side of a broken wooden cart. He rotated the dish, shouted through the walls of the ger to his wife, and when we walked back inside, the entire family looked proud.

Next to the incense holder, Destiny's Child sang "Bootylicious" on a black-and-white television. We watched the dancers gyrate, cameras spinning from navels to hips to the ripped abs of the backup dancers, until the entire room looked at me as if to say, "You live there? In that world?"

And suddenly my sense of belonging disintegrated. The broken wagon and the television powered by a car battery reminded me that I was just a tourist, with no idea what it meant to be a nomad at all.

After a year of work, I quit my job in Korea and wandered for several months through Southeast Asia. I started in Hanoi, traveling with another teacher.

I had my itinerary planned out. I knew what I wanted to see, where I wanted to go, how much time I wanted to spend in each city. I was sure of what to expect. I'd read guidebooks.

Three days into Vietnam, I'd been robbed twice, ripped off during a money exchange, had a postcard vendor try to sell me heroin, and spent the night on the floor of a slow-moving train that smelled like mildewed garlic. Somewhere on the train, I lost my guidebook.

We traveled to Mount Fansipan, on the Chinese border, with a plan to trek to the summit. But our guide didn't know anything about hiking. He lagged behind, chain-smoking. When I asked him whether he liked guiding in northern Vietnam, he replied that no, he hated it.

"I lived in Malaysia. That was the best job, at the factory. They gave me cell phones."

Near the end of our climb, the guide collapsed from heat exhaustion. We helped him down to the road, where we flagged a ride back to town in the bed of a logging truck.

The idea that a person could prefer work in a cell phone factory to walking through the woods unhinged me. I was young and sure I had the world figured out; I knew for certain that wilderness and faraway travel were the only paths to salvation. It didn't make sense that someone, anyone, could believe otherwise.

I think that was when my notions about wandering began to unravel. Asia became a muddled memory before I bothered to make sense of it. I moved quickly, retained only snapshots. In Vietnam, a water buffalo on a terraced hillside, a motorbike taxi driver who screamed "Fuck you!" when I declined his offer of a ride, the traffic. In Laos, a guesthouse on the Mekong River that sold marijuana milkshakes—we lingered a week before I left my friend in a hammock because I couldn't handle the catharsis. In

Myanmar, pagodas, a sand painting of Buddha that still hangs on my wall, cane liquor, cars burned to protest the junta. Beautiful photographs, skewed memories.

Perhaps the search for a life's meaning is like this: You are walking on a path through a forest. Side trails lead off in many directions, and you are plagued by choices. A wrong turn could leave you lost, so when the path you choose leads back to the main trail, you feel pleased with your decision. Thank God I didn't choose that route, you say. Look at those brambles. But suddenly you emerge in the parking lot and find that you wish to you could go back into the woods. After all the effort to discern the correct way, you realize that self-discovery and self-destruction follow the same route.

One night in Bangkok I shared a bottle with an Irishman and his Thai girlfriend, and when the booze was gone, I stood up on my plastic chair and demanded the musicians play "Freebird."

"Play some Skynyrd!" the crowd of expatriates chanted.

The next morning, I woke up on a plywood floor in a two-dollar hotel room and didn't remember how I'd gotten there.

I saw myself as a modern-day prodigal son, who could survive a crawl through the gutters and show up on my parents' doorstep to fanfare and a roasted pig. I didn't care about temples. I had no interest in learning about other cultures, no burning desire to ride around on elephants, laze on an umbrella beach, or volunteer at an orphanage.

None of my family knew where I was. I hadn't spoken to my parents in two months. The friend I'd traveled with through Vietnam had returned to Canada. My backpack contained a little climbing gear, a book of poems by Rumi, a pinstriped wool suit, and a bottle of moonshine stuffed with pickled scorpions.

I listened to other tourists talk about their visits to healing temples. I watched an American girl attempt to leap through a flaming Hula-Hoop at the full-moon party on Koh Pha Ngan. She suffered third-degree burns on her legs and crotch.

I hopped buses and tuk-tuks to the Malaysian border, then hitchhiked to Kota Bharu with an imam who picked me up on his motorbike. In Kuala Lumpur, I ate lunch with a woman who claimed to be a nurse. She coerced me into a gambling scheme that left me stranded far out in the suburbs. Eventually I took a ferry out of Surat Thani to the Perhentian Islands, where I moved into an abandoned jungle shack just off the beach. For most of August, I lay in a hammock, drinking and reading books borrowed from vacationers at the resorts farther down the beach.

I met a woman from New Mexico at a resort bar on the island and brought her back to my squatter's hovel. We followed footpaths out to where limestone bluffs met the sea. At three in the morning, we trusted the moonlight and leapt from a twenty-foot cliff down to the reef, hoping we were jumping at high tide. The next day, we awoke to find a nine-foot-long monitor lizard asleep on the porch of the hut; we crawled out the back window to escape.

The journalist and novelist George Alfred Townsend, who spent the last half of his life building an enormous estate in rural Maryland, wrote in *Lippincott's* magazine in 1891: "I took eight years at least, if not twelve, out of my life and invested it in experience, saving nothing, but going many a thousand miles that I might learn how to see; for the eye is to the writer what the hand is to the mechanic."

If you had asked me back then what I was looking for, I might have told you that I wanted to peer underneath the shiny advertisements and the perfect postcards. If I was a few beers into the night, I might have said I was trying to find a place where I felt like I fit in, though I doubt I could have explained what that really meant.

But ask me today: In all those months on the backpacker trail, studying the *Lonely Planet Shoestring Guide* like a bible, did I really learn some deep truth about my place in the world? Mostly, I was just another drunk kid on holiday, looking for a good story to tell the folks back home.

Years have passed since my Asia journey. Upon my return home, I fell in love with a woman in Minneapolis and tried to ground myself in more local pursuits. It didn't work. I took seasonal jobs almost compulsively—building hiking trails, fighting wildland fire, killing fish for a National Park research project. I even worked for a season at the South Pole. I lived mostly out of a backpack or at my grandmother's house. Eventually, I enrolled in graduate school in Alaska. The relationship I worked so hard to sustain from afar crumbled when we were together, and I found myself suddenly anchored to one place, and alone.

Like so many new Alaskans, a year in Fairbanks left me with a rescue dog and a growing collection of gear meant to help survive the winter. There was plenty of good summer work in the state, and I returned to firefighting for a couple more seasons. I hunted, fished, trapped, grew a beard. I wrote a thesis about my travels— about these travels—and read as much as I could about life in the Far North. For maybe the first time, I started to feel comfortable in my own skin.

Mollie, a fellow grad student and dog owner, lived close by, and we became friends. We went on skiing, canoeing, and hiking trips together. We met for beers to discuss our dating mistakes. It took more than three years, but our friendship evolved into romance, and after we both graduated, we moved together to the Lower 48. We walked for six months on the Appalachian Trail. We returned to Alaska and found work handling sled dogs. It felt like coming home.

Our relationship evolved again when we got engaged one day on a Cook Inlet beach. We bought a house, got married, settled into quieter rhythms. Mollie started a garden. In 2019 Mollie gave birth to our first child, a boy, and two years later, to a girl. When we travel these days, it's mostly to go on day hikes or visit family.

Sometimes I still dream of the cities and countryside I moved through during those years of drifting, but I no longer see them as exotic. I think about the strange looks people gave me as I walked through local markets, and I see now that it was me who was out of place.

The magnetic spin of the compass continues to blur for me the line between stability and chaos. Despite my best efforts, I worry that not much has changed. I have learned only that to be human is to take pause, to remember that sometimes we need to fail if we are to make meaning of what we have seen.

On that trip through Asia, I spent a week in the Cambodian capital, Phnom Penh. One day, at a bar called the Magic Sponge, I met an Englishman whose body was tattooed from throat to ankles. Dragons and tribal symbols and hidden meanings bled together in a mass of color. Mark proclaimed himself the only trustworthy tattoo artist in Cambodia.

"Why's that?" I asked.

"Well, quality and safety don't come cheap. If you want a good tattoo, you have to pay for it."

"How much are they?"

He said, "I start at twenty dollars."

The next day I visited his shop along the riverfront. Mark pulled out a couple liters of beer, smacked the caps off on the side of his workbench, and handed me a bottle.

"You want a tattoo?"

I thumbed through a few photo books. Mark complained about his Khmer competitors. He complained that there were too many regulations for tattoo artists in Britain. He punched the cap off another beer. I showed him a navigator's compass design I liked. He sterilized his equipment and drew a fresh needle from a sealed envelope.

A couple hours later, I blinked my way into the street, the ink turning to scabs between my shoulder blades. I was twenty-two and still worried about what might happen if my parents ever found out. Still, I felt safer with the tattoo than I had without it. The navigator compass, I had been told, acts as a talisman for sailors who fear they will never return. It could point me toward the familiar, to my father's shirts, smelling of sawdust, draped over a kitchen chair; to the family garden of my youth, filled with herbs and vegetables. I felt sure this tattoo could get me back home.

I flew back to Chicago after nearly eighteen months abroad, hopped the El downtown, and wandered into a coffee shop. There, I sat down next to a woman tacking away on her computer. I asked to use her cell phone. We talked for less than ten minutes before she presented me with a pyramid scheme: with just a little up-front cash, she could make me a fortune selling time-shares. It was the same story I had heard from every tout between Hanoi and Yangon, and I couldn't help but laugh.

The exotic, I had assumed, must be located somewhere else. I believed, stubbornly, that adventure required movement, and for a long time I ignored the signs telling me otherwise—the friends who settled into full-time jobs and stable relationships, the frustrated ex-girlfriend who needed me to slow down, the permanence of the ink on my back.

It has taken me years of living in Alaska—in one place—to realize there is not much difference between the forest and the city, between the tavern and the church, between the dead-end road and the tangle of thorns beyond it. In the end, a life well-lived resides along the boundary between the foreign and the familiar, tucked between the recesses of memory and the world we live in now.

Sometimes, in the dark of winter, if I lie still in my bed and focus, I can linger, just for a moment, in that fragmented moonscape where past and present intertwine. The instant I roll over, I ascend into a more graspable existence. I pull on my clothes, let the dog out, and fall into the routine of my day.

But I retain images of that other place, where I once lived in a surety of ignorance. I see a cigarette rolled with graphing paper, shared with a farmer at a stupa in Laos. I still taste the chemical burn on my throat. I remember my friend Jim playing guitar on a beach in Thailand for an American woman who proudly showed us her recent breast augmentation. "I saved, like, $5,000 on these," she said. I remember the day near Inle Lake in Myanmar when it dawned on me that the women who carried loads of firewood on their heads were not exotic. They were just poor.

When we reach outside the gray edges of our comfort zone, we can never crawl back into that familiar world and find peace. Travel, I now believe, is less a search for the fantastic than a search for a home. The sights along the way serve only to remind us of where we have gone. Our encounters with the unfamiliar teach us to understand memory: flashes of bright prayer flags on the steppe, the rot smell of durian fruit on a diesel bus, or the yellow light in a birch grove when the frost falls. One morning, we snap awake, we turn on the coffee, make an egg and toast, and as we sit down it occurs to us that those days are gone, and no amount of reflection can teach us how to proceed.

In Mongolia, Chuluun and I never found those missing horses. The coffee shop owner figured that somebody probably found them wandering with another herd and, needing meat, butchered and ate them.

"It is too bad," said the coffee shop owner, "but among the nomadic peoples, when life is difficult, we starve. That is life."

A few months after I left Phnom Penh, I used a mirror to look at Mark's work, and I noticed that the compass was crooked. Suddenly, it dawned on me that a compass can point in a thousand directions, and it was as likely to lead me into wastelands as to lead me home.

I've come to love Alaska—inhabited as it is by junked appliances—for its ability to teach stillness. In January when the temperatures drop and the car doesn't start, I step out onto the porch, and I think: maybe *this* is the land that will ground me.

I still get restless. Sometimes I strap on a pair of skis or snowshoes and just head out. I follow moose trails, flush ptarmigan, look for lynx tracks, wander into the black spruce and muskeg. Small pleasures that contain great rewards.

Perhaps the source of our fear and anxiety—the inability to trust ourselves—is the result of ingrained patterns. I bicycled through Turkey on my last long journey abroad, the summer before I moved to Alaska, and I had lunch one afternoon with an Australian I met on the road. When the waitress, who wore a hijab, informed him they didn't have pork chops on the menu, he shouted at her with embarrassing vehemence. Like me, he'd left home because he felt trapped by norms, but once abroad, it seemed like he couldn't accept a pattern of life so different from the one he'd known.

Maybe I haven't been any better than that Australian. The narratives I spin about my years of travel contain too many half-truths. I pretend I was searching for authentic experience, when in truth huge portions of my travels were spent sleeping off hangovers or wandering around trying to score some weed. I don't say: once, at a Mayan temple, I refused to pay a small child twenty-five cents for a walking stick.

Recently, while my son was down for a nap, I paged through old journals and found a memory. In Guatemala with my friend Wade, I forgot my wallet in a hostel. We bicycled through several towns and over a mountain pass before I realized it was gone. I wasn't even certain where I'd lost it. Still, I hopped a late afternoon bus back to the town where we'd slept the night before, and when I walked in the office of the hostel, the matron laughed at me.

"Ay . . . gringo," she said, shaking her head, wagging her finger. She handed me my wallet, credit cards, driver's license, and a full wad of quetzales still inside.

I had nearly forgotten this event, perhaps because those stories that have taught me to trust the goodness of others are too numerous to count. I have encountered such kindness my entire life. I did not need to go abroad to discover the humanity of others. I did not even need to leave home. At last, I realized: my travels to far-flung places were not the aimless wanderings of a prodigal son. I traveled because I had not yet learned to trust myself.

I am looking for a deeper ecology. When I search back through those wandering years, I find more and more holes puncturing the solidity of my experiences. I am glad my passport has seen few stamps this past decade. I have plenty to discover close to home—in the ineffable swirl of the aurora through the subarctic sky, in the trails of animals, in the intimacy of ghostly settlements half buried by the forest.

There is no cohesive narrative for our lives because, quite simply, our lives are not yet complete. A life well lived is a journey both wild and grounded, marked with memories and prayer flags, with an inked compass and a refrigerator shot full of holes.

On that Southeast Asia trip long ago, I ran out of pages in my journal and ended here: "The greatest conceit for a traveler is that the traveling never ends. There is always another place beyond the horizon that hasn't yet been tread."

Sometimes, in the fireweed summer or the yellowing autumn, Mollie and I sit in our yard and listen to the wind move through the trees.

The Fisherman and
a .410 Shotgun

O NE SUMMER SATURDAY in sixth grade, my father offered
to drive me fifteen miles down the road to go fishing with
an old man whose wife had recently died.

"John," my dad told me, "you'll make Mr. Radevich happy if
you do this."

"Sure," I replied, and rushed to our garage for my tackle box.

At age twelve, I held the opinion that there was no greater
pursuit in life than fishing, and I still believed that the whole
point was to catch fish. While my classmates watched cartoons,
I would don my father's waders and slog through icy streams
in pursuit of wary trout. On Sundays I brought a rod to church
because we sometimes stopped at a nearby lake on our way home.
The rest of the week, I spent hours in our front yard with a plastic
plug, perfecting my cast. I memorized the regulations for every
lake and stream in a three-state radius; I hid *Field and Stream*
articles in my school desk. I studied underwater maps with a
flashlight under my blankets, well after bedtime.

Whenever the chance to go fishing arose, I took it. It didn't matter to me that Dragisa "Jim" Radevich was seventy years my senior

or that his Serbian accent was almost incomprehensible. He was old, which to me meant that he probably had a lot of fishing experience. Logically, this improved my chances of catching more fish. Back then, I would have hedged almost any bet, suffered any embarrassment, endured any hardship, to catch more, and bigger, fish.

In junior high I still could not imagine a world where angling success might require more than the right gear and lucky bait. When my father took us on float trips down our local river for smallmouth bass or when we paddled the shoreline of some small lake while camping in the Chequamegon National Forest, it baffled me that he always caught more fish than my brother or me. For Dad, fishing was a flippant endeavor, something to pass the time while he looked for bald eagles and great blue herons along the shore. Though we had two perfectly good outboards stored in our barn, he mostly wanted to fish from a canoe. My arguments about how a motor could get us to better fishing spots were usually ignored. He viewed the water primarily as a place for reflection, and it frustrated me to no end that my father made catching fish seem effortless.

My family knew Mr. Radevich from church. As members of the Russian Orthodox Church, we drove thirty miles one-way every Sunday to attend a country parish founded in 1902 by a handful of Carpatho-Rusyn immigrants, where a handful of dairy farmers could chant Church Slavonic so mournfully that it brought the old folks to tears on Good Friday. Mr. Radevich was Serbian, not Rusyn, and had come to America after World War II. Our little congregation welcomed him anyway; in places where Orthodox churches are few and far between, cultural details tend to get a little mashed together.

I knew Mr. Radevich as the man who slipped five-dollar bills to me each week after communion as thanks for being an altar boy. I served behind the altar because I couldn't sing and because I liked the ritual of wearing the shiny robes—carefully folding the vestment, presenting it to the priest, bowing for the blessing. Now, more than twenty years later, I sometimes miss the liturgical ritual of serving. The effort to transpose a kind and practical spirituality elsewhere—to a successful hunt, to tying flies, to writing—has only rarely succeeded.

"You are goot boy," Mr. Radevich always told me, before he went out to the cemetery, in rain or snow, to visit his wife.

My father said Mr. Radevich reminded him of his grandfather, and I think his request that I spend the day with Mr. Radevich stemmed in part from this association. Dad, I think, imagined our fishing trip as a sort of character-building exercise. He treated church the same way—as a thing to endure. In my father's view, God was less a figurehead and more a conception of servitude. It was a view he learned from his grandfather, and he made it clear to me very early on that it is through servitude—and stillness—that we find faith.

For an impatient and restless kid, one who prays more to water than to God, the hardest thing in the world is to sit still. I know now that coaxing a fish to rise involves more than technique, but back then, I hadn't yet made the leap from religion to fish. It was Mr. Radevich who would show me the kinship with water that fishermen embrace, and teach me to understand something of my own weaknesses. Mr. Radevich would teach me that a great fisherman must respect tradition, put faith in God, and listen to the water.

←——→

Mr. Radevich stood on his porch when we pulled up, and he jogged over to open my car door. His shoulders were still strong; sagging jowls couldn't hide the square, high jaw or soften the reddened nose that turned almost blue when he drank brandy. Two cats crept into the bushes as we stepped out to shake hands.

Later in my life I would become a reader of fishing stories not for what they taught me about fishing but for what they said about the nature of obsession. I would discover that to fish was to experience a form of grace. I would learn to appreciate the beauty of a trout rendered in watercolor as much as I valued the quality of its flesh.

But that Saturday I sensed only that this old man shared my ache to have a rod and reel in hand. He, too, was an addict. When he unlocked the tool shed that held row upon row of fishing rods, stacks of tackle boxes, spools of line, oars and trolling motors and lifejackets, Mr. Radevich seemed just like me—an enthusiastic kid.

He pulled a few things off the shelves, and we went to load the boat. I was a small twelve-year-old, and he had an enormous rowboat, the hull scratched and dented, leaning sideways against a pole shed where he kept a flock of chickens. With no trailer, it was up to the pair of us—tiny kid and arthritic old man—to load the boat into his battered pickup.

We drove to Bass Lake. There are about four Bass Lakes near where I grew up; the one we chose banned the use of gas-powered motors. Mr. Radevich liked it for its relative quiet. I liked the weed beds where big bass surfaced to eat dragonflies.

Mr. Radevich insisted on running the trolling motor. We trolled along the shoreline, stopped at promising holes to try our luck. That day our luck was good. With Mr. Radevich's approval, I tied on a spinner bait—its hook tufted with feathers—and on the first cast, felt a hard strike. The fish ran deep, turned, broke the surface—a bass. I played it with slow turns of my reel. Mr. Radevich fumbled with the net, and when I brought the fish in close enough, he scooped it up.

"Goot job, Yon," Mr. Radevich said. His hands quaked when he helped remove the hook. I cast again. I snagged a decent-sized crappie. The sun beat down on the aluminum seats. It burned a little when I shifted my weight. This was paradise, I thought—like having a professional guide along. There weren't enough fish in the lake to contain my joy.

By the end of the day, we had a full stringer—several panfish, a nice sized bass, and the smallest northern pike ever to bite a line. Mr. Radevich had made me keep everything.

"Is okay. We keep to show you papa," he said, as we rough-housed the boat back into his truck bed and drove back to his house. We sat in the kitchen as I drank four full cans of Pepsi, enraptured by his thick accent and the fishing stories he told, while I waited to get picked up. When my ride came, he slipped five dollars into my hand and shoved a couple more cans of Pepsi into my backpack. I was beginning to suspect Mr. Radevich enjoyed taking me fishing more than he enjoyed fishing itself.

"Look at the fish I caught, Dad," I said on Mr. Radevich's front porch. My father was silent; he nodded. In the car, he raised his eyebrows and asked me, "Don't you think a few of those are a little under the size limit?"

"But . . . Mr. Radevich said I had to keep them," I protested. My father couldn't quite hide his tightlipped grin.

←——→

Despite his vigor, my fishing companion suffered not only from chronic arthritis but also from annual bouts with malaria. Mr.

Radevich had fought in both the African and the European theaters during World War II. He held opinions that seemed incongruous with his kindness—xenophobic ideas about race, religion, and game wardens.

Once, he spent a half hour cursing about a neighbor who had taken advantage of him. "This boy, he like to come to shoot foxes. But he drink too much. He drink four, five beer every time, then one day a case of beer. That damn boy—I tell him, 'you drink my damn beer, you don't come over no more.'"

It wasn't Mr. Radevich's job to give me a well-rounded perspective. He only wanted some company. Still, some of what he said bothered me. He didn't like Black or Asian people, or Muslims, Catholics, or Protestants. I wondered then, and still wonder now, why he shared such opinions with a kid.

In the years since his death, I have tried to dissect his stories, to separate the prejudice from the kindness, the lore from the real history, but what I have discovered has only deepened the mystery of his past. I want to see his words as instructional, or at least be able to disseminate meaning from memories skewed by time.

Once, searching for some way to corroborate my childhood recollections, I wrote to a priest who had often visited Mr. Radevich when his wife was still alive. "I enjoyed his goats," the priest replied. "He fed them cigarettes to keep them healthy." Of Mr. Radevich's war years, he knew little.

On the lake, Mr. Radevich told me that he had played professional soccer in Europe and South America. He had attended a military academy in Yugoslavia. When he mentioned his wife, his eyes filled with tears. He visited her grave nearly every day—a forty-mile round trip to the cemetery.

"Your family—it is good they go to church. It is important," he would say.

Mostly, I remember his stories about fishing: the day he filled the bottom of the boat with panfish or the twenty-pound pike he once caught below the Chetek Lake Dam.

"Fifteen people, they watch while I fight dees fish. Two hour it take me to bring to shore. But the meat is no good. I feed it to the cats."

Like all good fisherman, he exaggerated. Writer Nick Lyons says that in great fish stories "big fish are caught or lost; people say wild and spontaneous words; event becomes memory and sometimes, in the hands of a master, bleeds into art." The fish Mr. Radevich had caught were huge, impossible maybe. He always presented these stories—crappies as big as dinner plates, record bass, vicious muskies—as offhand, the same way he presented his past. And when we fished together, he rarely dropped a line in the water.

Still, if the memories of our youth guide our philosophical present, then I learned from this old Serbian the power of stories and the importance of faith. Faith, I have realized, isn't a moment of Zen understanding but a slow and tedious practice. Through faith comes grace and through grace comes understanding. We never fish the same water twice.

$\longleftarrow \qquad \longrightarrow$

Mr. Radevich had just one daughter I knew of, and she lived in Omaha. Except for the priest who visited him every few months, I was often his only company.

He succumbed to the isolation of his farmhouse. He gave up fending off the foxes and coyotes and let his chickens die. His garden filled with weeds. His house smelled of cat food, and Meals on Wheels delivered his dinner on Styrofoam trays. Cataracts clouded his eyes; it became harder to visit his wife's grave.

Our lives were like opposing mirrors. I joined track and dreamed about the girls' volleyball team. My obsession with fishing quieted. I neglected our friendship.

One Sunday at church, when he was still able to drive and I was just headed into high school, I asked Mr. Radevich when we could next go fishing. He complained about his arthritis but mentioned a slough not far from his house. I felt that sudden flush of unrealized potential, the kind that starts in the stomach and leaves your throat aching. The lake's obscurity, I thought, meant trophy fish.

"Only . . . very difficult to get in. My boat is no goot. Only canoe will work," he said.

"We can take my dad's," I said. He patted my arm and agreed.

A week later, my father helped tie the Kevlar canoe to the top of our station wagon, and at Mr. Radevich's house, I flung the canoe up over my head without any help and carried it down to the water.

The creek access to Moose Ear Lake wound through a maze of stagnant swamp. It didn't bother Mr. Radevich that he needed help getting into the canoe, or that we got lost multiple times, tangled in weeds and unable to pivot. He seemed just happy to be outside.

The sun burned hot overhead. A light breeze scraped at the tall grass. Milfoil swayed in the green August water. It was terrible fishing weather.

Once we had navigated the marsh grass, we paddled quietly, feeling less cramped on the open lake. I cast occasionally toward promising holes. For a long while we didn't speak. The fish weren't biting, and my thoughts wandered.

"Tell me about the war," I said. He didn't reply, and I worried I had offended him.

"War is no goot," he spoke finally. "You are goot boy, and it is goot you never know war . . ." his voice trailed off. I watched the funnels made by my paddle strokes trail off into the dark water. After a while, he began again. "I tell you. I was goot soldier. If I was young man again, I go . . . I fight these Moslem, these people are no goot," he said.

Mr. Radevich, even though he had not been back to Serbia in fifty years, was speaking of Slobodan Milosevic's atrocities against ethnic Albanians and Muslims, stories that appeared in the daily news.

Perhaps I shouldn't, but even now I remain tolerant of Mr. Radevich's bigotry. My memories of him are shrouded in a certain obtuseness, like when fishermen return with full stringers and say it was a good day but block out the slime and stink of so many dead fish. Perhaps it is my own willful ignorance that has allowed me to forgive his prejudice.

When Mr. Radevich next spoke, he did not mention current events. He spoke instead of his war, the World War. He spoke of horror, courage, and of the friends who had died next to him.

As a machine gunner in a fighter plane, he had been shot down during a battle over Italy. Though he survived the crash landing, Mr. Radevich was wounded. The only doctor they could find in the field hospital was a German prisoner of war. Someone held a gun to the doctor's head and promised that if Mr. Radevich didn't survive, neither would the doctor.

"I still have bullet, here," Mr. Radevich said to me, pointing at his chest. "Next to my heart, for fifty year now."

Behind watering eyes, shaking hands, and the pained wrinkles of his face, I tried to imagine the young soldier going off to battle. My childish notions of war and bloodshed dissolved; I found myself frightened by the horrors that had defined the life of my old friend.

We didn't catch a single fish that day. After a while, even I broke the golden rule of fishing—keep the line in the water—and stopped casting. Listening to Mr. Radevich speak of his history, I realized finally that for him, these trips had little to do with the fishing. Maybe I should have seen it all along, but I was a kid, and it took a day on still waters for me to understand that to fish sometimes means learning what it is for an old man to have lived.

The fall after I turned fourteen years old, I passed a hunter's safety course, and with that, my outdoor fantasies expanded into hunting. Mr. Radevich was the perfect man to stir this enthusiasm. While I casted for bass, he talked about shooting ruffed grouse, fox, and deer out of his backyard.

"One day, I see three bucks in dee field. One have ten point, one eight, and one have maybe twelve. Every night, they fight in the field. I shoot dee big one."

By then, a full day in the boat had gotten to be a strain for Mr. Radevich's health. We headed back to the truck early in the afternoon.

"We get back my home, Yon, you can shoot .22. I have priest from church, he love to come over, shoot gun with me. Now his family live in Cleveland. Every year, they send Christmas card. Nobody now to shoot with, so we try."

Back at his farmstead, he retrieved a rifle from his bedroom and showed me how to work the action. We set up a paper plate on a maple tree, and I spent half an hour shooting holes into the paper. Mr. Radevich smiled, satisfied. Back inside, he offered me something to drink.

"You want something? Pepsi?"

I cringed. Every time we went fishing, I came home sick from sugar, and besides, I hated Pepsi. He frowned at my pained look.

"You want beer?"

"Okay," I said, and I drank my first Leinenkugel's while he fed his two cats. We started talking again about hunting. Reaching into his kitchen closet, Mr. Radevich pulled out the .410 break action shotgun, his grouse gun. He passed me the weapon.

"Is it loaded?" I asked.

"No . . . no . . . is okay," he assured me.

I lifted the gun to my shoulder and pointed it toward the door. I cocked the weapon and took pleasure in the click of the hammer. Then I couldn't figure out how to release the action.

"Here, I show you," said Mr. Radevich. The cats slunk away along the flower-patterned wallpaper into the bedroom. "Uncock it, like thees," he said, and pulled the trigger.

My ears exploded as the shotgun blasted in the confined kitchen. I stared, mouth agape, at the shattered window. Shards clung like teeth to the pane, then crashed into the flowerbed outside. The room rang with eerie silence. Mr. Radevich looked dumbfounded.

"Oh no . . . oh . . . no, no, no . . . Yon!" he dropped the shotgun and gripped my shoulders so tight that I squirmed.

"You are okay? . . . is okay . . . no, no, no." He slumped down into a kitchen chair, and both of us looked at the jagged shards, all that remained of the window he had just blown away.

Slowly, our fright and confusion gave way to a guilty amusement. We went outside to look at the glass that had rained on his flower bed. After a few minutes, Mr. Radevich said, "You want Pepsi?" and everything was all right.

I was in college before I told my parents what had happened

to the window that day. After he died, I discovered Mr. Radevich hadn't even told his daughter. "He told me somebody tried to rob him!" she said to me at the funeral luncheon.

←——→

That was, I think, among our last visits. His health continued to decline; old demons caught up to him. When I visited, we just sat at his kitchen table and talked.

When he went into the nursing home, I didn't go to see him. I had started college and never seemed to find time when I was home for holidays. I knew he would have appreciated a visit, but I convinced myself that part of him would have been ashamed.

In my mind, I wanted to keep him as my fishing partner. So, I pretended he hadn't gotten old and that I wouldn't be missed. Perhaps, too, I wanted to hold on to my own memories of childhood.

The writer and fisherman Thomas McGuane believes our reasons for fishing have biblical connections. "The Bible tells us to watch and listen," he writes. "Something like this suggests what fishing ought to be about: using the ceremony of our sport and passion to arouse greater reverberations within ourselves."

The Book of Job mentions fishhooks. In Genesis, water came first. Izaak Walton, who in 1653 wrote the first guidebook on the pursuit of fish, claimed that fishing is the perfect merger of science and God. And I have found no better place to observe nature or to contemplate existence than from the bank of a river or on a lake at sunrise. There is an old cliché: better to think of God on the boat than to think of fish while in church. A nice sentiment, but I think Mr. Radevich would disagree. Better to think of God always, he might say—fishing is just a nice metaphor.

On all our trips, I never caught any fish big enough to brag about. The trophies I caught and the monsters that got away—

moments when the line broke or the reel malfunctioned or the trout slipped from my hands as I tried to bring it into the canoe— came at other times, fishing with my dad or my younger brother or a friend. Perhaps Mr. Radevich was not such a good fisherman, but on those trips with him, I was learning something infinitely more important. I was learning how to listen.

Mr. Radevich died around the time I graduated from college. At his funeral, I was asked by his daughter to be a pallbearer. I stood in the back of the church in the same pew Mr. Radevich had stood in for years and watched the altar boys concentrate on the dripping wax of their candles. I had done the same once; I knew how hard it was to stand solemnly for so long.

We carried his casket out to the graveside, to the plot next to his wife. As we laid roses and sprinkled handfuls of dirt with our parting prayers, I watched my father slip a five-dollar bill to one of the altar boys. That was one more thing Drago Radevich had taught me—we are expected, from generation to generation, to carry on the old traditions, in order that they be rendered anew.

After the funeral luncheon, I walked back out to the cemetery, where his casket had already been lowered into the ground. I crossed myself, drew a fishing lure from my pocket, and left it on the fresh-dug dirt.

A Clear Place in the Sky

Year after year it grew and was fed by its own brown
rotting, taller and denser in the dark soil of its own death.

—MARJORY STONEMAN DOUGLAS

*A*LONG THE SOUTHERN tip of Florida, the concepts of
water and land are indistinguishable. Murky backwaters
and deserted keys merge with mangrove tunnels and tidal flats
to create the million-acre labyrinth of Everglades National Park.
Herons, osprey, and alligators ply the creeks; tarpon and dolphins
hunt the bays. The air smells simultaneously like fresh sea and
rotting vegetation. Salt water and fresh water blur, and the ebb
and flow of human history in this place is—like the tide—held in
check by the vast swamp.

Mollie and I knew the Everglades was deep country. Even its
name contains mystery. *Glade* comes from Old English—meaning "an open area in a forest," or perhaps "stars in a clear sky"—
but look up the word today, and you will find a reference to south
Florida. In navigating a 150-mile route through a landscape so
dense that in places we would pull our way through mangroves
with our hands, inch by inch, I learned that in a salt marsh, the
quest for balance can be a delicate endeavor.

←———→

I like to tell people that I fell in love with Mollie during a blizzard in Fairbanks. Mollie lived down the road from me in a twelve-by-sixteen-foot cabin with two sled dogs and a heater that leaked carbon monoxide. She wrote beautiful, enigmatic short stories and dated stoic bearded men who seemed far more macho than me. One November a storm blew into town. In a fit of inspiration, I pulled on ice cleats and carried the makings for fancy cocktails over to her cabin. A few hours later, I left for home, rebuffed, tipsy, and wholly smitten.

Mollie tells a different story. She came to *my* house, she says, for a dinner she believed was not a date but that I worked hard to make into one. On arrival her dog Magnolia waltzed through the door, pranced up the stairs to my bedroom loft, and marked her territory on my bed. It seemed obvious to me that the dog knew what was best for her owner. Mollie, however, didn't agree, and so my affection remained unrequited for a very long time.

She finished graduate school a year in front of me and spent the summer in the Brooks Range. She asked me to look after her dogs for the last few weeks of her work contract. I said yes, of course. When her season finally ended, she announced she was moving back in with her parents in Georgia. Again, my hopes for a romance disappeared.

"Georgia's not far from the Everglades," I told her when I joined a group of friends gathered for beers before Mollie drove south ahead of the snow. I said I planned to visit family in Florida over Christmas break and that I wanted to paddle in the Everglades. She set down her glass, invited herself along, and spent the rest of the night showing me pictures on her computer from a trip she'd taken there back in college.

"You should know, I'll have to paddle in the stern," Mollie said.

"That's fine," I told her. "So long as I can steer from the bow."

Mollie arrived in Miami with a battered canoe strapped to the roof of her Subaru. The boat looked like it hadn't been on the water in decades, but she said she had tested it with her parents on the creek behind their home in Savannah. It floated, and that was good enough.

Sitting on my aunt's patio, the trip seemed like a great idea: navigate by nautical chart, paddle across sun-kissed bays, camp on sand beaches, and pull into Flamingo—on the east side of Florida—with big grins, toned arms, and tropical tans.

In truth, the entire excursion was a coping mechanism. I'd just ended another relationship, the latest in a long string of breakups that had defined my dating life in grad school. I was sorely in need of an adventure, even one through brackish marshland. This journey to the humid and haunted tip of the continent seemed, in a deluded sort of way, a perfect escape, and Mollie seemed to me perfect company.

I had been to the Everglades a decade earlier when I convinced my friend Alex, a good old boy from the hills south of St. Louis, to paddle the wilderness for spring break. I promised him we'd go to South Beach when we got out of the mangroves.

Alex studied German and anthropology because he liked the harshness of the language and because he liked cultures that did hallucinogens as part of their religion. He had a penchant for hard liquor and heavy metal, and every time he took out a new student loan, he would go to a crowded bar and buy the place a drink.

For our trip he got it into his head that we could find buried treasure on the shell mounds. To aid in this quest, Alex brought five liters of wine and a gallon of high-proof rum. By the end of our first day's paddle, we were halfway through the wine, had broken the camp stove, and when we landed at our beach campsite on Mormon Key, I passed out in the sand on my belly while Alex stumbled off into the palmetto brush.

We awoke in the morning with oozing bug bites and sunburns so bad it was impossible to wear a shirt. Two days later, my skin bubbled into liquid-filled pustules, which popped and dribbled mucus down my back with every stroke of the paddle. My skin peeled off in sheets.

Alex and I were young, stubborn, and could paddle into the wind for twenty miles a day and not have muscle spasms the next morning. When we emerged from the swamp a week later, we made a beeline back to Miami, where we followed other spring breakers from club to club for a few nights, and I forgot about the brutality of the Everglades.

On this trip, coming from Fairbanks where December temperatures drop to fifty below and daylight only shows up for lunchtime, I had less to prove and I wanted more space to think. I hoped the warm Florida air and good paddling partner could offer respite from the winter loneliness, a chance to clear my head of frigid cold and those bad relationship choices. I hoped if I could remember how to navigate the maze of tidal swamp, maybe I could navigate the rest of my life. At least that's what I told myself.

But you should never plan for what you go into the wilderness to learn, because you never find precisely what you set out to discover. We face the wild to see our fears more clearly, but in that place beyond the pale of family and bosses peering over our shoulders, it's not our fears looking back at us—it's our failures.

On New Year's Day, nursing hangovers from a concoction of cheap beer, limeade, and vodka—called gasolina—we'd drunk at a party the night before, we loaded our tent, lifejackets, paddles, two weeks of food, fourteen gallons of water, and fishing gear into Mollie's car and drove with my aunt and uncle to Everglades City. We spent an hour scanning routes on a wall map. We consulted a ranger, picked campsites, bought an extra bottle of sunscreen, and despite my aunt and uncle's pleas to try an easier route, we paddled off along the coast.

The Chokoloskee marina faded into one of those ocean sunsets that makes the world feel as if it's stuck inside a furnace. I rigged a fishing lure and tossed it behind the canoe.

In about two seconds, my rod tip doubled. I had a freshwater setup, and I struggled hard with that first fish. I had to look up in the guidebook what I'd caught —crevalle jack. It weighed just less than a pound. The silver body and yellow tail flashed neon when I released it. A minute later, I pulled in another. They kept biting, and I reeled in sea trout, red drum, ladyfish, and mackerel. Mollie made me put the rod away because I was catching too many. We wouldn't make it to camp before dark, she said.

We pulled to shore on the Lopez River just as the no-see-ums and mosquitoes swarmed, and here our idyllic dream ended. Mollie and I had both lived through Alaska summers. We'd felt the panic that comes on a calm day in the North when the mosquitoes rise off the tundra in swarms thick enough to kill a newborn caribou. We knew bugs.

But these no-see-ums were bad. They crawled into my ears, nibbled under my watchband, gnawed my toes, and tore at the corners of my eyes. It took an hour before we had killed all the insects in the tent. When morning came, my neck was swollen and the screened walls were smeared in blood.

To comprehend what it is to paddle through the largest contiguous system of mangrove trees in the world, take a piece of paper and give it to a toddler. Let them scribble on it with blue and green and brown crayon until the wax is thick and the colors blur. This will be your map. Here, rivers sprawl into mazes that offer no hilly backdrop, no shade in which to hide from the sun. You can't see a bay until you are in it, can't discern peninsula from creek from key until you have paddled miles in the wrong direction. In mangroves, there are no true landfalls, only tangled roots and graying leaves and muddy bays that froth when the wind picks up in the afternoon.

Even place-names in the Everglades seem sinister. Buzzard Key. Big Lostman's Bay. Camp Lonesome. Dismal Key. The Labyrinth. The Nightmare.

The Calusa inhabited this coast for generations. The Seminole Nation fended off the US government from bastions hidden deep in the inland swamps. These were the thickets where Ponce de Leon searched for the fountain of youth. Out here, the phrase "never find your body" doesn't seem like a bad line from a movie but the possible consequence of a stupid mistake.

The Everglades fluctuates with the tides; they determined how and when Mollie and I traveled. They shifted halfway through our second day as we paddled out of House Hammock Bay, headed toward the Gulf. Each stroke against the incoming tide became a battle against the inland sweep to sawgrass creeks and fresh water. After six hours, when our shoulders ached and the sun had branded us, the current flipped again, and a receding river spit us into the sea.

From the river mouth, we paddled toward a speck of land our map labeled Mormon Key, where Alex and I had collapsed years earlier.

Mollie wasn't convinced I was reading the map correctly.

"There's another key farther out and behind it. That one is Mormon Key," she said.

"Then what's this key closest to us?" I asked.

"Not Mormon Key."

We reached the island in an hour. A park service sign announced our arrival at Mormon Key.

"Go fillet your fish," Mollie said. "And I hope you get eaten by a shark."

Giant conch shells were strewn across the beach, some left there by the Calusa who had used them as tools long ago. We fried fresh sea trout in a mole sauce and ate while jogging up and down the beach to escape the bugs. When it got dark, I used a pocketknife to extract sand spurs from my feet while Mollie smeared mosquitoes along the sides of the tent.

An hour after dark, the raccoons came.

I don't envy the land animals that live out on the keys. The raccoons spend their lives thirst-starved, able to reach the mainland only by braving the mudflats, rife with the jaws of tarpon, hungry gators, and shifting tides. They eat mullet and pillage the coolers of fishermen, and in the later part of the dry season, the raccoons here will chew through a five-gallon jug just to taste a few drops of fresh water. Even well-aimed conch shells couldn't keep them from prying at our food box and spreading our dishes across the camp.

←——→

Mollie and I rode the crest of high tide back into the swamp and came upon the Watson house around noon on day three. One cannot read about the Everglades for long without finding reference to E. J. Watson, a farmer gunned down a century ago by a lynch mob that suspected him of murder.

In 1910 locals in Chokoloskee had discovered a body in the mouth of Chatham River. They accused Watson. He denied it. When he arrived in town amid the aftermath of one of the worst hurricanes in Florida history, a mob gunned him down as he landed his boat, before he could be formally accused.

In the century since, the shell mound plantation has been reclaimed. Sugarcane, run wild, stabs through the cracks in the old cistern. Mangroves have crept in. Gumbo-limbo trees and Jamaican dogwood cling to the higher ground along the brackish riverbanks.

E. J. Watson made cane syrup and kept his family here on the Chatham River. He planted banana trees, coconut palms, and a lemon grove. Once, he allegedly tried to slit a man's throat in Key West. He may have killed a man in North Florida. He may have also murdered a family of squatters camped on Turkey Key. Or maybe he was just a farmer. Nobody ever proved Watson actually murdered anyone. He blamed a worker from his farm.

The midday heat arrived, cloudless and still as a corpse, punctured only by the drone of cicadas. Pompano slapped across the Storter Bay flats. Ibis and herons waded along the shores. The tide kept rising, and in the late afternoon calm, the heat felt like a hot shivering through the bones.

Two fishermen motored up while we lunched at the homestead, the first people we'd seen since leaving Chokoloskee, but they couldn't make the afternoon feel less eerie. We left the remains of the homestead, buried under a tangle of honeysuckle and wild cucumber, to the ghosts. In this country, it takes a long time before history like that can get inurned.

As we paddled deeper into the glades, not even our paddles rippled the surface of the river. In the rising glut of seawater, I had the sensation that the tide was lifting me toward an inescapable radiation. We barely spoke, and it felt like ours was the only movement under a sun so relentless my skin felt translucent.

We steered among islands that manifested only when we paddled up on them and disappeared into the shoreline when I looked behind. The squiggles on our chart that marked our evening camp directed us into a narrow channel, barely discernable in the web of creeks and bays where a wrong turn could leave us lost for hours.

"Are you okay to navigate?" Mollie asked once, before we lapsed back to quiet. Even a whisper seemed to disturb the balance.

The air changed. We smelled fresh water. The tide kept rising. We reached the end of the estuary, where the river of grass and gator trails drained into the ocean by degrees. The day cooled, the ghosts retreated to the coast, and we spied the pair of palm trees noted on the margins of our map.

Night brought bugs, but it also brought relief from the sun. We camped on Sweetwater Chickee, an elevated wooden platform perched over the water with a tin roof that gave us our first shade since Watson's Place. Mosquitoes drove us into the tent at dusk, and we fell asleep early as a fog settled in all around.

Feeding mullet woke us the next morning, and through the

dense air, we watched a pod of bottlenose dolphins pass just feet from our platform, diving and squeaking and talking.

"Maybe they're protecting us from the ghosts," Mollie said.

Across the creek, a solitary alligator kept watch, and I wondered whether the reptile was a guardian or an ominous sign.

By the fourth day, we forgot there was a world outside the swamp. We fell into a routine: up for coffee, check the map, pack the tent damp with dew and the sleeping bags sticky with sweat, load the boat, check the map, lather sunscreen, check the map again, and paddle. A few hours' work, with careful navigation, put us at our next chickee.

For me, the time when we finished paddling was the hardest. The nearby mangrove formed an impenetrable thicket full of coral snakes, spiders, and fiddler crabs. I paced the eight-by-ten-foot platform, stir crazy, followed everywhere by the smell of the porta-potty bolted to the deck. My pacing drove Mollie crazy, and on top of that, she worried about the snakes.

"That looks like a python," Mollie would say of every gnarled piece of driftwood we passed.

"I don't see it," I'd tell her.

"You don't have any imagination," she'd say.

This was brackish water. It wasn't likely we'd see a python. Still, we knew they were out there. A few days before the trip, Florida had announced a month-long public python hunt—they offered cash prizes to whoever killed the most snakes and the biggest snakes. A week earlier, an Arkansas family had been picnicking at a rest area outside the park when a seventeen-foot python slithered into the gathering.

Pythons are not supposed to be in the Everglades. They aren't supposed to be in this hemisphere. In 1992 about nine hundred pythons blew into the Everglades when a Quonset hut full of them ripped apart during Hurricane Andrew. Pet owners release their snakes into the swamp, which happens to be a perfect habitat for large reptiles. Today, pythons have established themselves at the top of the food chain, and biologists estimate that they may number in the hundreds of thousands. They have decimated native populations of everything from rodents to alligators and endangered panthers.

Mollie and I debated who would win in a contest between a gator and a snake. We'd seen an Internet photo in which the alligator had been swallowed by the python before chewing its way out through the gut. It seemed like an even match.

Alligators were, for me, scarier. We hadn't seen many early on, but at the Lostman's Five campsite on the fourth day, I walked to the edge of the dock for a quick swim, hoping to rinse away the day's sticky heat. Fortunately, I looked before I jumped. An eight-foot gator lolled in the mud below me, close enough to see the jagged teeth and eyes.

"Mollie . . ." I said, "You're not going to like this."

Neither of us bathed the rest of the trip.

I hold a certain respect for gators. I like that they never really bothered with evolution. Sixty-five million years of ice ages and floods, birds and mammals and humanoids, and the crocodilian family has just hung around in wetlands, eating whatever new species happened by, not much concerned with anything beyond staying warm and fed. If a swamp dried up, they took to the sea until land reemerged a few millennia later.

When Mollie came out to see that gator, the mud swirled, and the gator swam halfway across the bay in an instant. They can survive in any habitat, from mangroves to sewers, and can eat anything from snails to black bears.

Our route also took us through the last refuge of the American crocodile. Only a few hundred remain on the continent. The far southern tip of the Everglades is the only place on earth where alligators and crocodiles coexist. And caimans live here now too—like the pythons, they escaped from pet owners and lurk in the canals south of Miami.

On the fifth day, we moved from the wide bays of the Ten Thousand Islands region—great currents haunted by E. J. Watson and teeming with fish—into the Central Rivers. Here, the swamp bore down so close you felt claustrophobic, even during the shadeless noon.

We caught the tide down Rodgers River and let it pull us toward the coast. We came upon a flock of roseate spoonbills perched in a gumbo-limbo tree, their outstretched wings glistening pink in the sun. Along a narrow stretch near the mouth, low tide exposed mudbanks to the sun, and alligators lolled in giant piles—four and five deep in places, climbing over each other, staring and snapping their jaws. We argued about the best way to avoid them.

"John, could you not cast your lure toward the gators? Please?" asked Mollie.

"I'm not casting toward them. There are gators all over the place."

"You are." We paddled on in silence for a half hour. The gators performed belly flops into the muddy water as we passed.

"I didn't cast toward them," I said at last.

"I know," said Mollie. "I wasn't mad."

These arguments occurred most often during the hard parts of the day. We cursed when we paddled against the wind. We shouted whenever an alligator surfaced too close to the canoe. We became passive-aggressive about reading the map.

"You don't trust my judgment," she'd say.

"I just want to see it for myself," I'd claim.

"I don't believe you. It's because you can't listen to other people."

"You're too sensitive, and you hate to not be in control."

Eventually, the tension would break. A flock of ibis would glide overhead, the tide would shift, and we would apologize. I wonder today if those arguments were also premonitions, lessons in learning to trust, preparation for the challenges we now face as parents.

"What am I going to do with my life?" Mollie asked one night, a cribbage game spread across the tent. She had been living with her parents for three months, and the strain was starting to show.

"Quit looking so hard," I said. "It'll work itself out."

"That's not very helpful."

Outside, the whine of mosquitoes pulsed like the ebb and flow of the tide. A turkey vulture squawked somewhere in the night.

"It's just . . . people must think we're crazy, coming out here to find ourselves," said Mollie.

When she had moved back to Georgia to sort her thesis into a book, Mollie had seemed optimistic. Now she seemed less sure. She said her friends in Savannah had grown up while she had been in Alaska. They had become doctors or lawyers or accountants, and they appeared well-suited to their ordered lifestyles. She said she was thinking about moving back to the North.

I told her I understood the feeling. It seemed like every choice I'd made in the past few years had been the wrong one. Wrong job. Wrong city. Wrong girlfriends. I'd lived for half a decade without a home address, and I was starting to get suggestions from my parents that maybe, since I didn't have a single publication, I should think about a different line of work.

I was almost thirty, and I should have spent this January working on my thesis project. I should have known I couldn't stave off loneliness by going on a trip with a woman I only wished I was dating.

We discussed our futures and fears for hours. If we woke up in the middle of the night, we shared what we remembered of our dreams. "I think mine was sexual," I told her one night.

"It was sexual." Mollie assured me. "You were making kissing noises."

Once, fleetingly, we considered a future we could share.

"I'm sure people think we're doing more than paddling out here," I said.

"You belch in your sleep," Mollie replied.

Fear feels different when getting lost isn't just the neurotic sense that your life is out of balance but a hard reality that can leave you stranded in the mud at low tide. That tangible fear is easier to put down. Just keep going; you'll see if the path is the right one soon enough.

On the nightmare route eight days in, the mangrove crept so close that fiddler crabs fell into our boat, and we pulled the canoe along with our hands to avoid the tangle of roots in our path. We joked that we'd get lost in walls of foliage, that we might be swallowed by the swamp or suffocated by the inescapable humidity, or that an alligator would bite the canoe in half.

Actually, I'm not so sure we were joking. Only when the waterway opened a little and a flock of great white herons exploded from the brush in front of the canoe did the tension release.

As we learned to live with the primordial fear of the swamp's dangers, we also learned to live in the moment. I began to feel privileged to be paddling through this strange ecosystem. It had, I knew, fended off a great many threats; it was fighting them still.

Take the birdlife as an example. A hundred years ago, hunters—known as Gladesmen—hunted for plumes here. They massacred anhinga and cormorants by the hundreds of thousands, killed egrets, herons, storks, and spoonbills by the millions, all so ladies in New York and Paris and Havana could wear feathers in their hats. When only corpses remained in the Everglades rookeries, competition for the plumes got so bad that hunters killed a local conservationist hired by the Audubon Society to protect the last birds. Oddly enough, though Watson was already dead by that point, some blamed him for that murder too.

In 1913, when only a few poachers were left to chase the few remaining birds, a pair of wardens described a massacre on Alligator Bay, which we paddled through on our sixth day. "Everywhere in the rookery, which covered several acres, we found the remains of dead long whites and a few of the spoonbills that had been shot," they wrote to *Recreation* magazine. "There were many little long whites that had died in the nests, and their bodies had been eaten by the buzzards. The trees were full of shot from the guns of the murderers, and the sight was the saddest one I have ever seen of the sort."

By 1900, 95 percent of Florida's shorebirds were gone. The populations today have come back, but not to those levels of long ago. On our journey, we saw only a few snowy egrets and even fewer spoonbills. We did, however, run into plenty of vultures.

The Everglades have a way of fighting back. When land developers introduced the Australian pine because it could suck water from the land, it worked wonderfully, and drained the soil from Lake Okeechobee out to the coast. Then Hurricane Andrew hit, and nearly all of the mature Australian pines were leveled. It turned out Australian pine doesn't do well in gale-force winds. Of course, in Miami, a group of shade lovers started a Save the Australian Pine movement and set about reseeding them back into the city parks.

Over a quarter of Florida's ecosystem is made up of exotic and invasive species. The water hyacinth can suffocate fish. The South American bufo toad has hallucinogenic toxins on its skin and can kill small dogs. The nests of monk parakeets have brought down power lines in the Miami suburbs.

There's more: the suckermouth catfish, the Asiatic clam, the lionfish, the walking catfish, cichlids, tilapia, and purple swamphen. Reptile catchers have found Nile crocodiles in the canals of Fort Lauderdale. In the 1940s melaleuca seedlings were dropped from planes to help drain the swamp faster. Researchers have found deer trapped and killed by the Old World climbing vine.

We followed the Shark River out into the western end of White-water Bay, where the Shark River Slough sheeted through the saw-grass into the ocean. Farther north, outside the national park, a mile-long bridge had been built over the Shark River Slough to allow for the natural flow of water to continue. This is the only part of a sixty-mile-wide waterway that still runs unimpeded from Lake Okeechobee to the ocean in its natural flow.

Most of the swamp has been turned into sugarcane and orange groves. Where once water ran in a great swath across an entire state, dikes now hold that water back for agriculture.

The Everglades is among the largest mangrove forests on the planet. It is America's only subtropical wilderness, and unless we can curb our rampant development, the Everglades may not survive. We have turned the river of grass into orange groves, turned the mangrove coasts into condos. In less than a century, most of an essential ecosystem has become a metropolis.

As we paddled, I considered what has been lost. On my first trip here back in college, when the mangrove roots had opened to the vastness of Whitewater Bay, it had been as if the world had opened with it. If I could hack it in this place, I had understood back then, I could make it anywhere. I never wondered what pursuing such dreams might cost.

It took this return journey to discover that shedding youth is not the same as gaining adulthood. Suddenly, I saw paddling the Everglades as a lesson in exercising caution. When the world unfolds before us, we must be deliberate in the path we choose, or we might find that the freedom we grant ourselves funnels us back to the same mistakes, again and again.

Our last few days were spent along the edges of Whitewater Bay, a giant body of water that stretches across twenty miles of inland coast. The name fits. Only a narrow mangrove buffer separates the shallow expanse from the sea, and incessant wind stunts the trees along the shore.

Wind opens a landscape. For the first time since Mormon Key, we felt the beckoning of ocean rather than the compression of swamp. We took the north side of the bay and paddled back to Canepatch, an old farmstead gone wild where freshwater gar swam under the dock and flocks of glossy ibis sailed overhead. That evening, we sweetened our water with wild lemons. Not far away, we spied the bulge of a manatee.

We timed the tides right and reached our next chickee by early afternoon. In the heat of the day, we lounged around, fishing and playing cribbage and watching birds wade along the shore.

In those moments, I thought I could stay in the wilderness forever.

I woke up in the middle of the tenth night chilled, sweating, and nauseous, a victim of dehydration and sunstroke. My head pounded; my body was racked by feverish aches. Bugs bit into the soles of my feet when I staggered from the tent to dry heave into the river.

"I'm sorry, Mollie," I said.

"Do you want some medicine?" she asked.

I took a long drink of water and rolled outside to throw up again.

"It's Pamprin," she told me.

"Period medicine?" Mollie laughed. I took the pills.

"Well, it works. Do you have any more?"

When dawn came, Mollie still couldn't quit giggling.

On our last full day of paddling, I saw a dolphin surface not far from the boat. We'd seen several pods of them along our route, mostly trolling for mullet along the shorelines, but this dolphin seemed different. I told Mollie, who was busy cussing at the wind in the front of the boat. Mollie loved to cuss at the wind.

"There's no dolphin," she snapped.

"I'm sure there was," I said.

"So where is it?"

It hadn't surfaced for a while, stayed underwater much longer than any we'd seen before.

"Maybe I was seeing things," I said.

Then it leapt from the water in a great surge, cleared its tail, and gurgled like a child. It leapt clear of the sea two or three more times, maybe fifteen yards from our canoe.

"He's showing off!" I said.

"She's beautiful," said Mollie.

For the rest of the day, we forgot to swear at the breeze.

On the last morning, we woke before dawn and paddled eight miles from Hells Bay chickee to Flamingo, across a Whitewater Bay calm enough to reflect the sunrise.

We celebrated the end with cold beers and ice cream bars and took our first showers in almost two weeks. Twelve days of sun, twelve days of wind and arguments and almost no ground to walk on, and suddenly the trip was over.

We hadn't thought up the next great American novel or discovered some important truth on the nature of love. We hadn't solved the mystery of E. J. Watson or found a way to keep the swamp from being drained and overtaken by invasive species. We hadn't even taken very good pictures.

Mostly we were still directionless, still unemployed, and still single. We had paddled along the edge of a continent and felt the cusp of an ever-rising sea, and I wasn't convinced that the experience had helped my sanity.

If anything, finishing made me feel a sort of kinship with the Gladesmen of long ago. For all their dreams of development, for all their destruction, they knew the power of the landscape. They poled through these bays for weeks at a time, and when they came to town with their loads of gator skins and plumes, it was only to unload and return to the swamp.

A hundred years ago, outpost stores stood on the stilts where remote chickees now serve as campsites. Egrets nested by the hundreds of thousands; families farmed Mormon Key and Gopher Key and Darwin's Place. A hundred years before that, Native Americans and escaped slaves established hidden communities in this wilderness, hiding from war and violence farther north. And three thousand years before that, the Caloosahatchee culture was building shell middens, creating land out of the sea over a span of millennia.

We had traversed an ancient Florida, a last bastion of wildness pushing back against the onslaught of Miami and Fort Myers, against the endless condo developments, against an entire society bent on believing that land is meant to be used instead of understood.

"Only when we put the outside world on hold," Mollie said, "can we figure out how to keep moving."

The closeness Mollie and I built in the bays and creeks had pulled something else to the surface: love. A few months after I returned to Alaska, Mollie drove up the Alaska Highway for a job as a dog handler, and our friendship emerged from its chrysalis. Our friendship became romance, then partnership, marriage, and eventually we became a family. The whirlwind of our lives together was born—at least in part—out of our time in the Everglades, the only environment of its kind anywhere on earth.

←——————→

When we returned to the city, night had already fallen. The starlit sky we had slept under was replaced by a dim electric haze; waves lapping against our chickee platform became a rush of engines.

The moment we left the national park, the sea of grass turned to fruit fields and traffic lights and highways, but the Everglades still felt close until we crossed the causeway into downtown Miami and drove past the Intercontinental Hotel. A seventy-two-story laser light display featured a woman with caricature breasts and hips, grinding up and down the entire side of the sky-scraper. You could see the show from the far side of Biscayne Bay.

Our skin had been burned tomato red. Our hair was tangled, headed toward dreadlocks. Even after showering at the visitor center, we still smelled bad enough that my aunt and uncle almost hadn't let us in the car.

Mollie leaned over to me in the back seat and whispered, "How long do we have to wait before we can go back?"

Desert Ghosts

*I*N THE HUNDRED-DEGREE heat, the men wore windbreakers. There were three of them, sneaking through a boulder field outside Ajo, Arizona, where I worked with my crew hauling concrete for the US Forest Service. The men ducked around rocks, used scrub oak and oversized yucca as cover while they descended the dry wash down to the desert and north toward Tucson.

When I saw them, I crouched behind a mesquite tree. It was an instinctual reaction, made before I considered who the men might be. Smugglers? Migrants? I felt like an amateur birdwatcher, or a Peeping Tom—a voyeur. I felt suddenly ashamed because of my impulse to hide, but before I could stand, the trio vanished into the dry expanse. I looked south down the valley toward Mexico, worried more people would follow. None did. The men had disappeared so quickly that I wondered after a while if they had been a mirage.

◄———►

In 2008 I spent nine months along the Arizona-Mexico border, working as a crew leader for Southwest Conservation Corps and later as a wildland firefighter in a mountain town in the Tonto

National Forest. By the time I left, the borderland had become a place that both obsessed and terrified me. I felt troubled by the region's complicated past, peppered with Franciscan priests and Confederate mercenaries who came to convert or enslave the Indigenous people who have thrived in this dry land for millennia, and with those Mexican and Apache revolutionaries who used hidden Puebloan ruins as last sanctuaries in desperate bids to reclaim their stolen land. I felt even more disturbed by the present, where drug wars, anti-immigration militias, and proposals to build a wall through the desert have become facts of daily life.

But I was haunted most by people who didn't seem to exist. I walked in their footprints and sifted through their garbage; I found their traces among fields of marijuana plants my fire crew burned after a Drug Enforcement Agency bust. I saw them from a distance, heard their voices and movements in the bushes. Their lives, their journeys through the desert, scared me; working along the border, I never found a reference point from which to take an accurate bearing. The world there only made me spin. As the years have gone by, it leaves me ungrounded still.

As Americans we celebrate our history as a nation of immigrants. We learn as children that our legacy of colonization gave opportunity to untold millions and carved a civilization out of the wilderness. My own great-grandparents came to live in northeast Minneapolis around 1920, settling in an immigrant neighborhood where they could still speak their native language. My grandmother knew only Slavonic as a child and didn't learn English until grade school. My parents, aunts, uncles, and cousins still refer to the Old Country with a kind of reverence.

An aunt who has made a hobby of family ancestry recently

traced my great-grandmother's arrival to this continent through Nova Scotia. Of my great-grandfather, she could find no record. He most likely arrived illegally. In a story my father tells, my great-grandfather was once asked to show identification at the Canadian border while on a family vacation. He didn't have the papers and so was forced to walk back across the bridge to the Michigan side of Sault St. Marie. I imagine him, by then a diminutive old man, afraid everything he had built would be torn away, that he would be trapped alone on a bridge between worlds.

An estimated eleven million illegal immigrants live in the US, though their numbers are difficult to calculate. The politics of immigration—how to address the influx of people, how to determine whether they belong, how best to manage this invisible population—seems increasingly volatile. Yet from some perspectives, namely those of the first occupants of this continent, nearly everyone in North America is living on stolen land. We reap the benefits of past pillage and plunder and still have the audacity to decide who gets to move in next door.

I came to work for SCC—a nonprofit organization that partners with government land-management agencies to promote conservation efforts in the desert—because I was broke and because I knew how to build hiking trails. I moved into a grimy apartment on the southwestern edge of Tucson and shared floor space with six other people. We slept on camping mats and listened to our neighbors get into one domestic fight after another, as first the man, then the woman, were hauled off to jail.

At the end of our block, a burrito stand sold carne asada and tamales. I used broken Spanish to order, struggling to remember forgotten vocabulary from high school. A nearby strip mall boasted a *carnicería* and *panadería*. I shopped at the Super King grocery store, where six varieties of chili peppers, pig heads, and prickly pear fruit were piled in among unfamiliar canned goods. One weekend several of my crew members went down to the Mexican side of Nogales and returned with black eyes. They'd been beaten and mugged at knifepoint only a few minutes after they left US soil.

The Sonoran Desert is a scorched landscape, a place desperate and transient and beautiful, a place where at first glance only brittlebush stands out. Tumbleweed shakes in the wind like arthritic claws, weathered by the sun. The rocks are a refuge for Gila monsters, horned toads, kangaroo rats, and thirteen species of rattlesnakes. In spring, poppies blanket the gravel hills for a day or two, pollenate, then die. A dozen species of cactus give sanctuary to javelina, roadrunners, ringtail cats, even the occasional jaguar.

In wilderness, we want to believe that we can hide the scars of our exploitation. We set aside space to protect against the onslaught of our newcomer mentality. But look closely across this emptiness. People making the crossing from Mexico mark their passage not with what they seek but with what they leave behind. As have we all.

A month into my job the Bureau of Land Management hired our crew to pick up garbage dumped in the desert by migrants at the end of their journey, where they loaded into vans and bounced along ranch trails toward the state highways that led north to Phoenix and Tucson. The BLM had spent months searching for the site we were to clean. They nicknamed it "Big Boy."

The cleanup was funded by government grants and was run mostly by a woman named Emily Hertz. Relying on GPS, she spent days wandering the wide-open expanse, driving through washes, and walking miles among desiccated peaks to locate a dump site. In her two years working along the border, Emily had unearthed several locations to clean up.

Big Boy was fifty miles from the border, hidden on the north side of the scorched Tucson Mountains. It seemed unreal that anyone, let alone women with children, or children traveling alone, could make the trek over such jagged peaks. Yet here, at this dump site, clandestine travelers who had endured the passage were loaded into cramped vehicles by *coyotes*, smugglers who transported people through the desert for a price. After months of travel, their journeys ended in the dead of night, often being chased by border patrol or rival gangs of human smugglers or even groups of civilians "protecting" the borders with hunting rifles.

For our own crew, reaching the garbage cleanup site required seven vehicles, all four-wheel drive and government white. Rangers escorted us along a bumpy two-track. My clenched fists cramped while we drove through sandy washes and thorn-covered branches brushed against our van. Once, a border patrol helicopter flew low overhead and tipped a rotor in greeting after it determined we didn't pose a threat.

I had imagined this job would be like picking up trash along a highway. I pictured a few beer bottles, cigarette butts, some empty food cartons, maybe a shoe with no match, an old tire or two. I was wrong.

←——→

When we arrived at the Big Boy site, park rangers with assault rifles and flak jackets spent an hour securing the area before we could hike a third of a mile off the rocky, gullied road to begin work down a nearby arroyo. We took the delay in stride, loitered around the vehicles, waiting for the all-clear message to come over the radio.

Once the area was secured, we hiked in, spirits high; we cracked jokes about hardhat hair and discussed ideas for dinner. Two people made evening plans to build and fly a kite.

Then we crested the hill, and we fell silent. Along the ridge, hanging in trees, speared to cactus, draped over razor-edged yucca stems, strewn along the dry ground were the belongings of tens of thousands of people. Several acres of ground were invisible, buried by people's lives, flung out to bake in the desert.

I stood transfixed by a swath of possessions that had no way to hide. Here, miles from anywhere, it felt as if I had stumbled into a void, a scene so gruesome it made me nauseous, a place caught between an awful ending and a sad beginning.

Slowly, fighting an urge to run, I waded into the sea of trash. I began picking up Pedialyte bottles by the hundreds, the plastic crumbled and faded. Together, our crew collected tubes of toothpaste, toothbrushes, maxi pads, medicine bottles with the labels still on, high-heeled shoes, toddlers' shoes, baby clothes, used diapers, unused diapers, leather jackets, canned beans, shirts, bras, prayer cards written in Spanish with faded icons of the Virgin Mary or St. Christopher, pamphlets about safely crossing the border distributed by Christian churches on the US side, and spent bullet shells.

I helped remove blankets, dirt-encrusted crucifixes, human excrement, cheap makeup, a punctured soccer ball, used syringes, pornographic cartoons, photographs unrecognizable after weeks of exposure to a sun that bleaches everything to bones.

Hispanic tradition holds that garlic keeps the devil at bay. One afternoon I pulled a large head of garlic, cloves shriveled and skin flaked like burnt parchment, from under a creosote bush.

Scientists have found that some creosote plants can live for ten thousand years; here, a dozen of them grew scattered like a fire-scented orchard among the trash. Crouched low, the smell of ash and garlic mingled in my nostrils. The garbage was choking these plants; several bushes had already died. Somehow, the sweet odor reminded me of cremated remains.

To track the number of people coming through the region, the BLM asked our crew to count the backpacks we collected. A sort of dysfunctional government census. We tallied over two thousand. Our statistics did not, could not stop this movement, could not predict futures, could not convey a sense of tragedy in this vicious cycle. With every tally in my pocket notebook, I felt as if I were erasing a human being. Clearing this trash was environmentally responsible. I understood the hazards. Yet the act implied that neither we nor the migrants were a part of this land, and each backpack taken from the ground ushered a ghostly feeling into the arroyo.

A coworker said, "It's like we've created our own sick ecology."

More than once I came across torn women's panties hanging on a tree; a sign, Emily said, that coyotes, or bandits, may have raped a woman there. Apparently they would fling the undergarments into the brush, making sure they were visible as a mark of their conquest.

We unearthed a journal written by a young boy, with poems that told of his passage from Central America. I tried to imagine a small child walking here, feet blistered and punctured by thorns.

One of my crew members went to the Tucson Public Library, translated excerpts of some of the poems, and found the location of the boy's hometown. He'd come from a village in Honduras. He did not write his name in the book. He was fourteen. I wish I could find that boy today and return his journal. I want to give him back his secrets.

I remember the first time I saw the border, along the southern edge of Big Bend National Park in Texas. I was nineteen and had never seen desert before. Huge skies soared over dry sage flats. Craggy peaks hung on the horizon. I was struck by the desolation, the strange, lifeless appearance that belied a tenacious world living in the shadows.

A friend and I drove for a day and a half to reach the border country. We hiked high into the mountains, among pinyon pine where black bears roamed and views stretched into the Mexican state of Chihuahua. It was impossible to distinguish what land was Texas and what was Mexico. Somehow that surprised me. If I could not discern Mexico on the landscape, how was it different from my own country?

After two days traveling down through hills and desert washes, we reached the Rio Grande. On the American side, we found an abandoned mission church surrounded by palm trees. Two hundred years earlier, this had been a village. Now only the broken adobe and a stained hot-spring pool remained.

I thought at first that we were alone, which made the nearness of Mexico seem enthralling. I had always imagined the Rio Grande to be a wide, flowing river, pouring millions of gallons through a great basin, but the river was less than twenty yards across. I forded the river, and the current came only to my knees; I shouted to my friend that I felt like an immigrant.

He pointed across the water to the Mexican side, where a man sat on a broken lawn chair. A woven sarape served as a roof for his shelter. A blackened pot bubbled over an open fire, dangling from a tripod of sticks. I left the border country a day later, filled with questions and reeling emotions.

Our crew worked nine hours a day for five days, clearing the mess at Big Boy. We hauled debris to the road, where we filled trailer after trailer. We struggled to fathom hundreds of these dumps, stretching from California to the Gulf of Mexico, mummifying in the dried mud. Most locations are never found. How, with an average of seven hundred thousand people arriving illegally each year, can we possibly cope with the impact this migration has on the fragile desert landscape?

Twice we were called away from Big Boy because a UDA (undocumented alien) was spotted. No arrests were made, but the idea that we were being spied on unnerved me. The threat of being stranded because someone might steal our government vehicles was very real. A missing truck had been recovered recently only because someone noticed the bluish-green vehicle, painted the color of the Forest Service, was mislabeled; it had Park Service stickers on the sides.

The BLM rangers were mostly ex-military who carried a weapon in one hand and a plastic trash bag in the other. They seemed to really care about our work, and despite their body armor, they worked alongside us in the heat, hauling three or four trash bags at a time, maintaining their patrols even during lunch breaks. I think we all sought an empathetic language to explain the experience, and I think it eluded us.

In arid environments, movement defines a species' survival. When presented with the harsh realities of an unforgiving landscape, people across the political spectrum seem to forget the glaring inhumanity of a place that must involve real people. Human laborers build the walls that will exclude others from those same labors and opportunities. To clean the garbage felt almost like an avoidance technique, as if by clearing the trash, we could pretend these migrations did not occur; that the human presence, however disturbing, was not a part of the history of the desert.

The border we imagine is different from the border we come to know. Here, the environment determines fate. Desert life requires a willingness to move on when the water runs dry and the food grows scarce. The Sonoran's vicious beauty—angry peaks and valleys capped by a sky of unrelenting yellow-blue that rises each morning from pencil etchings of sunrise and fades fast each night into cold purples and pinks and golds—does not recognize borders. Like the plants that have developed a certain toughness, residents of the desert must adapt or die.

After a few days at Big Boy, the garbage lost its horror, lost even the charm of novelty. Our energy returned. I found myself whistling when I carried full bags along our beaten path back to the trailers. The crew began to hold contests: Who could carry the most bags? How many backpacks could we gather in an hour? We learned to ignore the cigarette butts, diapers, bottles, the unused condoms and the used tampons, the tattered clothes and broken shoes and tin cans half full of molded tomatoes.

One afternoon, a ranger named Sarah gathered the crew around a spindled ocotillo bush, where she held a two-foot-long, buzzing reptile.

"This is a tiger rattlesnake, the smallest but most venomous rattler," Sarah said. "I call all snakes Bob, after my ex-husband, because they bite."

When nobody else volunteered to hold the snake, she shrugged and released it. The snake hissed and slid under a mound of dried toilet paper.

By the end of the week, we could think of the area in business-like terms and began to use phrases like "project efficiency" and "productivity increases." Our evenings again filled with laughter. Once we had a sing-along, accompanied by guitar.

One evening Emily talked with us about her years spent immersed in this work. As she spoke, it seemed we settled some sort of score, came to terms with the sensorial emotion of Big Boy. She highlighted the myriad problems facing immigration policy: Latin American politics; the impossibility of separating drug trafficking from human trafficking; small children found wandering thousands of miles from home in search of parents; a fence that allows nothing larger than a rabbit to pass through but which still cannot stem the flow of people. When pressed, she, too, recognized that simple solutions to deal with this border are hard to come by.

"Why are you so dedicated at finding these sites?" someone asked.

"How do you feel about immigration law?" asked another.

And one person wondered, "If we clean it all up, what's left?"

Discovering that Emily, despite her passion for border issues, had no easier answers to these questions than we did seemed to help our crew accept the absurd nature of the work. The aridity, the desperation, the sad and comical wildlife among the trash, became more fun anecdotes of the work season.

We cleaned up the entire area in five days. The belongings of people who had made the perilous journey were thrown into black bags, the bags counted, hauled away, and discarded in a proper landfill. Only when the garbage was almost gone, piled high on a pair of farm trailers, did I finally begin to feel comfortable in the arroyo.

As time has passed, I've built a family and come to believe that roots grow from us into the land. We must be willing to see the place where we live for what it is, and not for what we want it to be. In the many years since I worked there, I have not returned to the border country.

When the garbage was gone, I wondered if we'd somehow severed a last cultural connection. Those who had passed through hid themselves well, but in that world of ill-defined boundaries, their lives—strewn about and covered in balls of cholla cactus— were already forgotten. Today, I wonder: who was intruding on whom?

In truth, it wasn't the initial shock of what I witnessed in the desert that made the job difficult. Rather, it was the feeling of accomplishment when we had cleaned it all up, a feeling that we'd returned the area to the wild, and having done so, could go back to the city and forget.

I spent my last evening at Big Boy sewing a minor-league baseball patch I had found—the team was the Aguilas—to my backpack. I liked the idea of sports fans bringing memorabilia on their journeys, and I wanted this patch as a remembrance.

The gesture fell short. When the final scrap of debris had been hauled away, an area that once held the secrets of thousands belonged again to no one, and when it seemed no human had ever trod in those arroyos, the ghosts emerged. Nothing I had learned could make the place feel less haunted.

Discovering Terra Incognita

As far as the eye could see, there was nothing but an icy
shroud, white ruins, *tabula rasa.*
He hadn't a minute to lose.
He was going to populate this wilderness.

—BLAISE CENDRARS, *Dan Yack*

B EFORE I LIVED in Antarctica, I still believed it was the last
place on Earth left to explore. I grew up reading Robert
Falcon Scott's journals, tracing routes from the Palmer Peninsula
to Queen Maude Land on a map in the front of the book. In the
Minnesota Science Museum, I stared for hours at photographs of
calved glaciers. I would spread a map of the continent across my
bedroom floor and trace my finger along the coast. I memorized
the names of landmarks—the Gamburtzev Mountains, Vostok
Station, the Pole of Inaccessibility, the Dry Valleys, the Queen
Maude Mountains, the Mertz Glacier, Casey Station, Vinson
Massif—and I always, before folding it along worn edges, traced
the longitudes to their intersection. South Pole, it read, labeled
in bold.

So when Raytheon Polar Services hired me as a general construction assistant, even though I knew the title meant glori-

fied snow shoveler, and even though I understood the job would be thankless, I still imagined I was joining ranks with those explorers who came South in search of glory, greatness, and self-actualization. I expected to feel lost in an untried landscape. I expected the wind and cold and the glare of never-ending sun. I expected the people I worked with would be the sort who fell naturally to the fringes of the map. But I never guessed that the bottom of the world would be quite so—weird.

In the final days of October, I flew to Denver for training—tedious corporate lectures held in warm classrooms imbued with the promise of the Earth's southern terminus. After four days of deployment paperwork and company protocols, Raytheon put me on a plane from Denver to Los Angeles, then to Honolulu, Sydney, and finally Christchurch, New Zealand. In a building near the airport, I was issued two duffel bags of ECW—extreme cold weather—gear. I sat in a hotel room for three days waiting for the weather to clear over the Southern Ocean. At last I reached the Ice: McMurdo Station, the last layover before my flight to the South Pole, and my first view of terra incognita, the unknown land, Antarctica.

$$\longleftrightarrow$$

Ice appeared hundreds of miles ahead of the continent, great chunks floating closer and closer together until I peered through the portholes of the C-17 cargo transport plane onto a white so white it made my eyes ache. I fought to discern the contours of landfall and, slowly, the clouds tinged gray on their edges. I noticed striations far below—crevasses and ascents of the Transantarctic Mountains—and when we began our descent to the sea ice off Ross Island's coast, I glimpsed long fractures, snow-packed ridges, and pockmarked blue ice blown barren by the polar wind.

We landed in late afternoon. Fifty of us, dressed in red parkas, bunny boots, and ski goggles, stepped onto the Ross Ice Shelf at 77.51 degrees south latitude. Snow feathered its way to crystal-line horizons; sea and land merged with sky, dancing together in bloodless miasma.

The thermometer read eighteen degrees below zero; cold sunlight circled the sky. A mile away, station buildings sprawled— tan and green, stark and industrial—up the smoking side of Mount Erebus. Along the distant shore, where the Victoria Range jutted out of McMurdo Sound, the only color came from black volcanic rock and the atmosphere's pallid blue arc.

A century earlier, Sir Robert Falcon Scott set off on his doomed expedition from this same spit of land. His hut, still standing and pristine, was visible a mile away on Cape Evans. Colored flags checkered the ice, marking the roadways and runways across the pack. The old explorer shack, the red of our parkas, the growling of construction equipment, and the station—with its two taverns, coffee shop, visitor center, and decommissioned nuclear power plant—felt pathetically impermanent, like a surreal painting where the sense of scale has been created with overwhelming white space.

Standing on Antarctic ice for the first time, I felt like an intruder. It was as if I had departed from earth. To simply survive here seemed like a postapocalyptic existence. To feel and smell the reality of 12.4 million square miles of frozen expanse, to place upon a scale the fathomless weight of that much ice pressed upon the earth, left me winded. The land—and my mind—felt as if they had been flipped upside down.

Ice crystals bit into my eyes, a pressure ridge thrust blue ice onto the edge of the runway. I caught a whiff of jet fuel from the plane, watched as it lifted into the sky and headed back north to Christchurch. We climbed into a transport vehicle—the name "Ivan the Terrabus" imprinted on its side—and bounced toward the station amid a rumble of machinery, voices, and crackling sea ice. The pleasure was maddening.

←——————→

> I have felt all the time that the diet of dog does not agree with me.
>
> —DR. XAVIER MERTZ, MAWSON EXPEDITION, 1911

The Antarctic Plateau doesn't warm enough to land a plane on it until the end of October, so although I'd been hired to work at South Pole Station, I spent two weeks at McMurdo, scooping snow off diesel pipelines and reorganizing drums of oil in an old freight canister out near the abandoned power plant. Except for an overnight survival training course, where we simulated polar blizzards by walking around with five-gallon buckets on our heads, I spent the time after my shift ended shuffling between buildings to attend nightly science lectures. I visited the library and taverns, sent postcards to my parents, and played cribbage over glasses of red wine in Quonset huts.

One afternoon I hiked out to Cape Evans and visited Scott's hut. Rows of books still sat as they had for a century. The shelves were lined with canned meat, fish, vegetables, and a few hunks of preserved seal. A pipe rack for his several smoking pieces rested in the corner. The hut felt like a museum display, the supplies like impossible attempts to stave off homesickness. The scene struck me as ridiculous. Pork rind and a chessboard couldn't make Antarctica feel like the green pastures of England. That much, at least, was obvious. I zipped my parka against a stiffening wind and walked the mile back to the base.

That evening, at the coffee shop and tavern, a pair of workers sat in a corner, playing a guitar and a stand-up bass borrowed from the station's music room. In the next building over, people exercised on treadmills and Stairmasters after their workday. In the dining hall, they were serving pad thai and massaman curry for supper. It occurred to me: the incongruousness here reminds us that our efforts to tame Antarctica are themselves absurd. In a landscape where nothing is familiar, superfluity is essential. We can't cope without it.

←——→

I lived in limbo while I waited for my flight to my real job at the Pole. Really though, it was worse than limbo, because I stayed in Man Camp. When they distributed keys to all new arrivals on the first day, I was left standing with two other guys in the hallway.

"We, uh, didn't get keys," I said to the woman in charge of orientation. She looked at my paperwork and giggled.

"Your room doesn't have a key. That's Man Camp."

"Man Camp?" I asked.

"You'll see," she said, and called to a welder in the doorway. "Hey, you want to show these guys Man Camp?" The welder laughed.

Man Camp was designed as a one-night layover for workers passing through to other stations on the continent, and as such could hold nearly fifty people who, as per policy, all happened to be men. The thermostat blasted heat twenty-four hours a day, keeping the room at a consistent ninety degrees, but when I opened a window to cool off, I woke up in the morning with frost on my eyebrows. I spent the nights feverish, my nose numbed by cold, my feet damp with sweat. A climatologist sleeping in the bunk next to mine was also bound for the Pole. He managed to get on the season's first flight, but I was on the manifest for flight nine or ten.

One night a group of Australians passed through on their way to Casey Station, drank their last hard liquor for the season, and passed out on whichever bed they happened to trip over. I returned that night to a naked, snoring Aussie in my bunk. I slept in the hallway my second week.

←——————→

Polar exploration is at once the cleanest and most isolated way of having a bad time that has been devised.

—APSLEY CHERRY-GARRARD, *Worst Journey in the World*

The roads of McMurdo are made from wind-pummeled volcanic rock. After a few days of walking around, people began to take on the same gray appearance as the land. Soot covered the sides of buildings. Rows of steel pipe, transporting diesel, water, electricity, and excrement, surrounded the station like a fence. The dreary appearance of the station made the unblemished wild outside the perimeter that much more alluring. We sought the warmth of taverns to escape the diesel smell that saturated the air around town.

One day my friend Emily and I skied out onto the Erebus Glacier. We stopped at the fire station, checked out a radio for emergencies, and glided across the ice. Every ten feet, red and blue flags jutted up from the Styrofoam snow, and zigzags of black ribbon denoted hidden crevasses. Halfway up—a bulbous hut stocked with food, sleeping bags, and stoves—served as a survival shelter. When we reached the outcrop at the top of the route, the vista exploded out before us.

The view in Antarctica relies on a skewed perception. Moisture on breath turns instantly into ice crystals, but it is not simply that you can see the steam. Exhalations seem to sit suspended in the rarified air, and on sunny days, the atmosphere shimmers with millions of microscopic flashes, a hoarfrost with nothing to cling to but exposed skin and hair. Occasionally, the crystals linger long enough to glimpse a flash of rainbow. Once, deep in the tunnels under the South Pole, I controlled my breath while holding a cupped hand under my chin. In the beam of my headlamp, I watched the vapor hover in the still air for a moment, then fall in visible shards onto my glove.

On the glacier, Emily looked out at the Ross Sea along the distorted horizon and said, "My favorite color is white. Once you've seen ice like this, white never seems plain . . . there are so many different kinds of white it blows my mind."

I attended sea ice training. Several people, decked out in ECW gear, climbed into a tracked vehicle and lumbered out toward Razorback Island several miles up the coast. The wind was light—we could see four or five flags in front of our vehicle. We zipped by across bare ice, snow whipping sideways toward the distant Dry Valleys. As we paused to take a depth sampling, a lone Adélie penguin waddled and slid into view. In a month, three hundred thousand more would arrive at Ross Island, but on this frigid spring morning, open water was fifty miles distant, and the bird appeared as a gray speck, a comma on blank paper.

In October, air force transport jets land on the sea ice, but by January, McMurdo Sound becomes open water peppered with icebergs, and excursions such as ours become impossible. The sea dissolves into a jigsaw puzzle of jumbled floes; migrating whales, seals, and birds flock to Ross Island in a cacophony of sound. After less than two months of summer, the super-saline currents that surround the continent push polar air back down, and katabatic winds will blow down from the glaciers. By late February, life flees back north and darkness returns.

On the way back to the station, our vehicle, called a piston bully, stopped by Razorback Island to visit the breeding grounds of Weddell seals. A hundred blubbery blobs bleated and wallowed in their own afterbirth along a rift in the sea ice. Not far away a glacier extended out from the land, and we climbed into a crevasse that had burst open a few hundred yards from shore. Above me, two hundred feet of ice churned its way out from shore—in the silence I imagined I felt the bobbing of the tides. Impulsively, I licked a tendril of ice; it froze to my tongue, and for a moment I was gripped by a fear that the glacier might calve.

The last dregs of the long winter clung desperately to the coast, making flights to the Pole irregular and dangerous. Workers and scientists filtered through Man Camp, a summer populace spreading across the continent. My desire to escape McMurdo grew. Because I didn't have regular work, Raytheon made me a lackey. I filled out time sheets, set up army tents, organized lumber, and helped build a mini-golf course for a carpentry shop costume party. I attended the event dressed as Ziggy Stardust. Three bands played on a rough-cut stage; other partygoers dressed up as pirates, penguins, scissors, krill, and the Blue Man Group.

McMurdo—despite the roughly one thousand inhabitants, the bars, the yoga classes, the seals and penguins—made me feel masochistic. I wanted more cold and fewer people. I wanted endless white space and a spinning compass. I came to regard the station as a tiny stain, like an abandoned cabin in a wilderness or rover tracks on the moon. McMurdo acted as the last outpost on the edge of the map, but I hadn't yet fallen off the bottom. Besides, after a week of sleeping in a hallway, colder, windier, and more bizarre didn't sound too bad.

At last I was to leave for South Pole Station. On the last day, I met a New Zealander while I climbed to the top of Ob Hill, a half mile from the station. We talked about our jobs, about the sacrifices and philosophies that had filtered south. I told him I was headed to Pole, to shovel snow.

"Not too many people can say they've shoveled snow in Antarctica, mate," he said.

Across the Sound, Mount Discovery shimmered in the month-long sunset. A handful of seals, looking like spackled black dots, lay strewn along a distant pressure ridge. I checked my watch, buttoned my parka, and turned back down the hill to catch my flight.

$$\longleftrightarrow$$

In 1911 the only extraneous item Roald Amundsen carried on his quest to the South Pole was his journal. The Norwegian had by then spent three winters held fast in Arctic ice. He had walked five hundred miles from the Beaufort Sea to Eagle, Alaska—and back—to telegraph news of his successful traverse of the Northwest Passage. He had survived in barren country and had found colonial sensibilities ineffective for polar travel. Amundsen meticulously planned his bid, considered every step from Norway to the bottom of the world. A plaque on the wall in South Pole Station notes that his sled dogs gained weight on the journey.

The Amundsen Expedition arrived at 90 degrees south latitude on December 14, a tired outline set against a backdrop of unceasing white ice, where sky cannot be discerned from solid ground.

"So we arrived and were able to plant our flag at the geographical South Pole," he wrote, claiming the world's southern axis for himself and his country.

A month later, Sir Robert Falcon Scott and company turned up, wasting away from malnutrition. They had brought ponies to carry them to the Pole, but the first horse died on deck two nights after setting sail from New Zealand, and none had survived the voyage. Neither Scott nor his companions would make it back from the Antarctic Plateau alive. Eleven miles from his supply depot, a rescue crew found him frozen. "The Pole," he had written. "Yes, but under very different circumstances from those expected."

Triumph and tragedy.

We trickle south in search of a perception unachievable elsewhere. For decades historians have been obsessed with an alleged recruitment ad for Ernest Shackleton's 1912 *Endurance* expedition that advertised a "hazardous journey, small wages, bitter cold, long months of complete darkness, constant danger and small chance of success." Supposedly, more than five thousand people applied, and Shackleton spent months selecting his crew from the pool.

That the story is most likely a fabrication says a lot, I think, about our collective conception of Antarctica. By mythologizing those who venture into those strange southern latitudes, we skirt the threshold between imagination and reality. Consider: Recently the US government sent me a civilian service medal as commendation for the work I did in Antarctica. On the back of the medal are inscribed the words "Courage, Sacrifice, Devotion." In that liminal space between danger and desire, I shoveled snow.

Perhaps for some—the intrepid and legendary explorers and today's possessed polar workers—the inexplicable pull of the Pole stems from the sufferance of a magnetic drive. I still, on occasion, long to return to the icy continent, and I still wonder: if a life's meaning is found atop 9,301 feet of ice, how will I ever find a place where it feels like I belong?

$$\longleftarrow \quad \longrightarrow$$

> And so you will travel nearly alone, but those with whom you sledge will not be shopkeepers: that is worth a good deal.
>
> —APSLEY CHERRY GARRARD, *Worst Journey in the World*

Those who live and work at the South Pole, whether dishwasher or astrophysicist, approach the ice with a sense of awe that borders on religious conviction. I met architects who quit high-paying jobs to load cargo, scuba instructors hired to clean toilets, and a poet who drove a forklift. A woman who had grown up as a bear hunting guide on the Alaska Peninsula dated a lobster fisherman from New England. They'd both been hired to install siding on the station.

My job was simple. Every winter blowing snow consumes any place left open to the elements—every hole, every ventilation duct, every gap where even a screw works loose. Mountains develop between the massive sub-ice fuel storage tanks. Drifts obliterate entire buildings. Each summer season a mile of storage materials, organized in rows called "the berms," must be uncovered. Raytheon hires a small army of workers to dig out the buried items and help with odd jobs.

For four months, I dug out boxes of station garbage, uncovered four-meter-tall stacks of random metal pipe, cleared snow off sheeting and L-brackets, bales of wire, old tires, lumber, T-shirts, and frozen lobsters. I spent a week tucked under the floor of the station's storage arch, bolting shelving to the floor by hand. The temperature in the crawlspace where I worked never fluctuated—it remained a constant thirty-five degrees below zero. The outside air temperature often wasn't much better. We dug deep channels into the ice cap and ran hundreds of meters worth of electrical cable; we used chainsaws to cut blocks of ice away from the station's pillar supports. I shoveled out telescopes, wind generators, latrines, and forgotten military rations, all—as we reminded ourselves again and again—in the name of science.

Scientific research at the South Pole is, for the most part, pretty esoteric. Telescopes measure ions in the upper atmosphere; meteorologists study weather behaviors to predict global climate changes. Those who support these projects, "Polies," as we are called, are meant to believe that this research places us at the vanguard of scientific discovery. The entire station becomes, in many ways, imbued with the sense that grand and mysterious things are at work here.

We cannot perfectly describe the experience of a world where earth and sky are indistinguishable, but we may be able to measure it. The largest scientific project in Antarctica during my time there, IceCube, was part of an attempt to quantify and trace an unfathomably small subatomic particle—the neutrino. A grant from the National Science Foundation allowed for the building of a square-kilometer telescope buried a mile and a half into the ice. Thousands of basketball-sized sensors measure the rare reactions of these particles and trace them to their origins in galactic nebulae.

What little we know of neutrinos makes their potential all the more powerful. They are among the most abundant particles in the universe. A German scientist explained to me that, "Every second, a billion neutrinos pass through the nail on my pinkie finger, but across an entire lifetime, they may only react once in the space of a living room." One day at dinner this scientist admitted to me his hopes for the project—that with IceCube, we might pinpoint the Big Bang's location in the universe. Another visiting physicist, after a talk one evening, said, "The statistical improbability of the Big Bang having actually occurred on any sort of universe-forming level of explosive photonic reactions is so remote that nothing but divine influence could explain its existence."

These opinions—that by use of a scientific method we might discover the divine, and that the IceCube project places us on the cusp of this discovery—seem a uniquely Antarctic sentiment. The lines between theory and reality become blurred, perhaps because we do not yet understand this polar landscape. We have experienced the physicality of the Antarctic for just over a century, and it remains difficult for us to believe that an entire landscape exists where the only perceivable entities are imprecise—there must be more than simply ice and light.

I assisted in installing the wires for the IceCube telescope. For a week we used an ancient snowmachine to drag nearly $30 million worth of cable from the cavernous holes they had been lowered into, each hole drilled with pressurized water, consuming seventy-five hundred gallons of jet fuel to dig deep enough, to the two-story computer room that would monitor the reactions.

I spent two days in the fetal position while the cables, a thousand feet long and as big around as my arm, were positioned. As snow blew around in eddying gusts, a dozen people heaved these cables through a drainpipe to the second-story balcony of the computer building. When a tug rope broke, it sent everyone tumbling backwards into the pooling drifts of snow. We almost destroyed the whole computer system.

←———→

> One comes to measure a place, too, not just for the beauty
> it may give, the balminess of its breezes, the insouciance
> and relaxation it encourages, the sublime pleasures it offers,
> but for what it teaches. . . . It is not so much that you want
> to return to indifferent or difficult places, but that you want
> not to forget.
>
> —BARRY LOPEZ, "INFORMED BY INDIFFERENCE"

Around Christmas, workers gather to watch the arrival of the annual fuel traverse. Fuel use at the South Pole in the summertime exceeds twenty thousand gallons per week and requires an expensive type of jet fuel. AN-8, used only in Antarctica, is transported either via cargo plane or by Caterpillar operators who drive eleven hundred miles from McMurdo towing giant gut sacks of fuel on custom sledges.

Occasionally skuas, Antarctica's aggressive scavenger gulls, will follow the fuel traverse all the way to the Pole, where they circle for days, disoriented, desperate, and unable to escape, before succumbing to exhaustion. Along with Amundsen's flag, they are buried by the snow, entombed by ice for the next hundred thousand years. Life here can only be buried.

A strange mythology has worked its way into the South Pole Station's culture. Each season, workers uncover objects that reinforce an odd respect for the brief history of the station. For example, one day we found a stash of bacon bars left over from when the navy had managed the station in the 1970s. After much debate, we tore open the packages and ate them in homage to the station's history. They were salty, basically bacon bits pressed into the shape of granola bars. A pipe insulator and weightlifter named John, who had worked at South Pole for more than seventeen seasons, remembered when boxes of these bacon bars had filled whole shelves in the old station.

One day a dozer operator broke through the upper crust of snow and fell, machine and all, into the dining room of the original station. The structure had been abandoned and buried since 1959 and had migrated fifty yards from its original location. After the operator had been rescued, he told his story over a curried chicken dinner.

"It was crazy. There were still plates of food on the tables and coats on the benches. If we heated the steaks back up, they'd be edible," he said. Eventually, they retrieved the bulldozer and filled the hole, entombing those stories in the old dining room forever.

A former winter-over worker shared a story about the psychological effect of the South Pole without sunlight. After two months, one employee began compulsorily turning off every light in the station. When he started shutting off the dining hall lights while people were eating, a group of coworkers responded by installing flashbulbs in front of his bedroom door. The man took his meals in his room and refused to speak to anyone until the sunlight returned. Nobody could quite figure out why, when the only illumination came from the aurora australis, he spurned even the glow of a light bulb.

Toward the end of the work season, a flight tested the ability to airdrop supplies in the event of a winter emergency. We watched the plane buzz over, and later the boss told us a box of bread flour failed to deploy its parachute and exploded over the snow. After work, I went out to search for the location. I glimpsed a speck near the horizon I thought might be the shattered crate. A friend and I trudged across the flat landscape toward this lone blemish. After two kilometers, we arrived to find only a sastrugi ridge, pockmarked wind deformations in the icy crust. The box, if there had been one, was covered, the flour sifted into the atmosphere and dispersed across the continent.

Our stories mimic the heroics of the early explorers. Like Scott, it does not matter that we are at best unprepared, overzealous amateurs. We want to believe that our myths are true—that an Australian actually died after drinking glycol filtered through a sock (supposedly, he'd heard the Russians at Vostok Station made vodka that way)—and they may be. Certainly, strange things do occur, but for me, the provable moments feel most important to understanding my time in Antarctica.

The axis of our world shifts several meters each year, a slight wobble at the pivot point of the planet. Every New Year's Day the words of Amundsen and Scott, inscribed as epitaphs at the geographic South Pole, are ceremonially moved to the newly measured, precise bottom of the earth. The station manager, and perhaps a visiting explorer, recite the triumphs of humans over landscape and embed a marker, newly commissioned each year, on the new site. It is a reorientation of the indiscernible.

The South Pole smoker's lounge is famous for wild parties and thirty years of undissipated cigarette haze. The lounge comes complete with a stocked bar, a handful of regulars, and a stripper pole for when parties get wild. At one such party, a naked electrician used a plumber as a snowboard and rode him down a pile of excavated snow berm outside the doorway.

We drank beer stored in cans for over half a decade. Many of our station chefs had left jobs at world-renowned restaurants to deep-fry tasteless vegetables stored for a decade. On clear days, halos and sun dogs encircled the ever-present sun. A tourist from China flew in for a one-day visit and developed heart palpitations upon his arrival. A group of us who held mostly expired First Responder and EMT certifications monitored his vitals for twenty-four hours before he was airlifted out. He had departed from Punta Arenas, Chile. When he awoke, his plane was bound for New Zealand.

The lack of bacterial life sucks odor from the air, and after four months of sweating in bunny boots, the only smell that emanates comes from spilled jet fuel. To get drinking water, a steam drill melts ice fifty feet below the surface. This same water, reprocessed as waste, is dumped into hewn ice caverns. Giant stalactites of gray water stab up from the cavern floor, the crystallized shit of an entire station, buried into the ice cap.

The mean annual temperature is 57 degrees below zero Fahrenheit. The coldest temperature at the South Pole was recorded June 23, 1982: it dropped to 117 degrees below zero. Even in summer the temperature never rises above zero. In the wintertime, a sort of impromptu club forms. To gain entrance, one must turn the station's sauna temperature to 200 degrees Fahrenheit and endure the searing heat for several minutes; then, on a particularly cold day, pull on shoes, dash for the Pole, touch it, and return to the sauna. The sprint is clothing-optional, and those who succeed enter the "300 club," for having endured the extreme oscillation of temperature.

←——→

Who are the chairbound to belittle men of hardihood, however driven, foolish, incompetent and even without scruple some may be? What is this awful need we have to

pull the brave ones down into the mob by exposing their
human frailties and mistakes? Are we so incapable of peace
within ourselves that we find the eminence of bolder men
unbearable?

—PETER MATTHIESSEN, *Ends of the Earth*

The terra incognita of our minds has not disappeared; it merely,
like blowing whorls of snow, perpetually alters itself to fit the
shifting boundaries of human awareness. We must be reminded
that there is as much value in what Antarctica promises to
teach as there is in what we have come to learn of the place.
These paltry striated spaces, the organized human outposts of
Antarctica, are defined by latitude and longitude, by meteorology
and scientific measurements. Today, the continent is understood
not through the glorious mythos of explorers but through the
quantifiable strictures of science. Yet Antarctica will always be
a frontier, and despite what we understand, the frigid beauty of
that ice-shrouded world remains as mythical as ever.

One of my favorite paintings is a work by the artist Xavier
Cortada, on display at South Pole Station. It depicts the bust
of Shackleton, wearing dirtied yellow suspenders, his face
benevolent and tough but blurred by the thickness of the paint
on canvas. In the top right corner are the coordinates of the most
southerly point the explorer reached. The materials for the work
were gathered on the continent and include crystals from Mount
Erebus, seawater from McMurdo Sound, and soil from Ross
Island and the Dry Valleys. How fitting to our conceptions that
these natural materials depict a constructed and foreign object to
the Antarctic landscape, that the image is displayed in the place
that eluded its subject for a lifetime.

The South Pole offers a place for the imaginative to form theories on the origins of the cosmos, but the truth is that other places on the continent are far stranger. More inaccessible, hidden by frost, they exist in the realm of story and make up much of the folklore that defines our brief presence on the continent.

The Dry Valleys of the Central Transantarctic Mountains are known for the scattering of mummified crabeater seals strewn across the ice-free valleys. Scientists fly by helicopter to the Valleys each year to measure the decomposition rates of the trapped and frozen remains. Decades of wind eventually curve their bodies and freeze-dry their skin and, like burned paper, the seals drift apart in chalky fragments.

The world's largest unfrozen lake rests below three miles of ice cap under Vostok Station. The Gamburtzev mountain range is over nine thousand feet above sea level but can only be mapped using sonar, for the peaks are still buried under a mile of ice. I once talked to a pilot who had flown a Twin Otter over the Pole of Inaccessibility, the farthest point from the coast and the most remote spot on the planet. He claimed that an enormous stone statue of Lenin had been erected there by the Soviets and that the bust still stuck up from the snow.

←——————→

Working each day in the cold and wind, I became accustomed to lifelessness. Scientific presentations, musical concerts, and a visit from Sir David Attenborough distracted me from the tedium of an imageless landscape. Only when I arrived back in New Zealand did I understand how the deficient nature of the polar world had affected me. To emerge from a place that belies understanding is to realize its importance. Antarctica, it would seem, contains the potential to connect us with the imagined landscapes of our souls.

For me, the unfamiliar and harsh desolation is a strange solace. I have sought it elsewhere, but never quite felt the pure release of spirit associated with the Ice. Only the southern polar plateau offers an absolute nothing. In seeking a clearing of the mind, Antarctica's interior contains the sole opportunity for a known landscape to share in scouring clean our mind's excesses.

I remember the night before I flew back to New Zealand, in the bright 3 a.m. sun, a moment when the bulldozers, snowmachines, and airplanes, the wind and snow even, fell silent. This glimpse of a complete serenity brought me to my knees; I realized the potential of ice.

Antarctica demands to be spoken of differently. I turn to the penguin pair huddled on the ice for advice on survival. I imagine the mummified seals of the Dry Valleys embracing the dry wind on their skin for eternity. We can learn to encounter desolation with a given joy.

Once, when most workers were asleep, I sat alone in the station sauna until the heat had worked deep into my organs. Then with a whoop, I crashed through the storm doors into the everlasting daylight. In seconds my skin was a sheen of frost, every hair grasping to retain the warm moisture, lest it escape to the dry plain. My feet pounded the snow, needle points stabbing my heels, crystals freezing my eyelids shut. A bulldozer had plowed the surface into a gradual hill, and with a leap, I rolled downward. My sides and legs chafed against the ice, rubbed raw as if they'd seen sandpaper. Before I returned to the station, I scooped a handful of blown powder to my face and rubbed the ancient elements into my hair.

Into the City of Jasmine

I ENTERED SYRIA THROUGH the port city of Latakia, on a ferry from Cyprus that no longer operates, and I stayed my first night in a hotel that, as best as I can tell, has since been destroyed.

It was evening, July 2010, the summer before the Arab Spring, and I walked my bicycle through the terminal and onto a main thoroughfare lined with date palms. The air hung heavy with the aroma of black tea and exhaust. Kids kicked a soccer ball around a vacant lot. Couples strolled along the boardwalk, holding hands. Below, coils of razor wire wound through the rocks where the slow break of the Mediterranean lolled against shore.

All of Latakia was celebrating the World Cup, and although Syria hadn't even made it through the qualifiers, car horns cheered on the teams that were still playing. Apple-flavored hookah smoke rose in plumes along the street. Euro-pop songs played from a distant window.

On my first night in Syria, I listened to the rhythm of that music for a long time, as if the bassline held a clue to help me understand why I had come. I experienced a traveler's conceit—that here, amid the duality of headscarves and miniskirts, the illegal Internet cafés and Koran sellers, the burger joints and open-air spice markets, the concrete high-rises and ancient ruins, I could find a sort of tranquil balance, and perhaps even locate my own lost faith in God.

Now it is too late, and trying to make sense of a country's happiness more than a decade into war is a frivolous task. My memories of welcoming people and serene cities feel like lies. My photographs of an antediluvian countryside confuse me. All I retain are disjointed scenes from a vacation on a bicycle, recollections burdened by guilt, as if I am sifting through the photographs of a smiling family days before a fatal accident.

I think: I was young, selfish. I wonder: how could I have been so deluded?

The most common reason for travel—wandering as a means of escape—is probably the most foolish. I decided to ride my bicycle from Istanbul to Damascus because my girlfriend broke up with me two weeks before we were to leave for a trip through Greece. Heartbroken and stuck with a plane ticket, the thought of two months sitting on the sunny islands where I had hoped to make a marriage proposal depressed me. I decided that instead of blue-domed Orthodox churches, I would pedal past the blue-domed minarets of Turkey down into Syria. In 2010 the region had not yet hit a critical level of chaos, and my friend Bassam, a Syrian American, suggested that his family in Damascus would love to have me to visit.

I knew bicycling alone through a foreign country was a dumb way to get over a break-up, but I sent off my passport to the Syrian embassy anyway. I journaled about the decision to ride east—I had discovered a claim that Turks and Arabs harbor a collective melancholy, something they called *hüzün*. I wrote that the idea fit my mood. I imagined a holy land, filled with people who understood my faith—people whose languages I didn't speak, whose religions I actually knew little about. My notes conjure up lonely deserts and Gnostic prayers. I believed I would find balance in anonymity and escape. I even called the trip a pilgrimage.

In the many years since that solitary journey, I've learned to be more honest about my motivations. When we broke up, my ex-girlfriend told me, "You don't make me happy." She didn't explain.

Even today, as a husband and father, her statement still haunts me. When Mollie and I argue, the seeds of doubt reemerge. I think: I'm not good enough. Old fears claw at me—my hyperactive energy, my lack of focus, my impulsiveness, the narrative about ADHD I've fought most of my life. Back then, the idea that I was the problem in the relationship triggered a flight response; I wanted to go somewhere edgy, somewhere not wholly safe, somewhere a little bit dangerous. It has taken me a long time to admit, but I went on this journey because I was angry.

My break-up left me questioning the role of my faith and, more importantly, my sense of belonging in a community. Most of the relationship had been long distance; I saw myself as a traveler and I'd rejected any suggestions of settling in one place together. I'd spent much of the relationship trying to justify my unending desire for new horizons; I'm not sure I ever listened to what she wanted.

Suddenly I was alone, and maybe more than who I wanted to spend my life with, I wanted to know where to spend it. Somehow it seemed easier to reconcile my doubts, to grapple with my core beliefs, and to think about where I fit in while traveling among strangers in a place I didn't know.

The arrogance I must have had to believe I somehow belonged in the Middle East. Now I know there is nothing more egotistical than an outsider who thinks they understand the locals. The landscape, I wrote, had healing properties. The travel was more authentic, the people kinder, the politics more nuanced. In my journals from that time, I find a manufactured exoticism, the stereotypical condescension of a Westerner in the Orient.

My visa arrived thirty-six hours before takeoff, and I flew to Istanbul. I spent a few days in the city and a few weeks pedaling through Anatolian wheat fields. I hopped a ferry to Cyprus and then took another boat to Syria.

A student on the ferry approached me as we waited for customs agents to arrive.

"You have American passport?" he asked.

I said I did. He laughed.

"You will wait. But it is likely they will give you tea."

South from Istanbul, I took a ferry across the Sea of Marmara and pedaled into the Turkish interior. Movement brought a sense of release, and I traveled in a haze, marking my days by the number of small towns I rode through. I ate at gas stations and sat at plastic tables on street corners. I contemplated the scenery and the burn in my calves as mountain passes descended to broad fields of wheat and rose again into more mountains.

The landscape did little to unravel my loneliness. Rather, it seemed to embody my emotions. When the muezzins called to prayer in the towns where I stayed, I imagined I was sharing a religious experience. I wrote: "It is the sound of those who mourn because they can never draw near enough to God to hold his hand." I was describing my own melancholy.

In Konya, I watched whirling dervishes perform in the city arena. I searched for talismans of ancient Christianity along the edges of the highway—an ancient monastery on a hill, abandoned for centuries; the glass-encased well at the birthplace of Saint Paul, where actual pilgrims elbowed me out of the way to taste the holy water. Time and miles slid by. I made note of the strange sights, smells, and sounds, but I never stepped out of my own head long enough to notice my appropriation.

I spent several days in the city of Mersin, along Turkey's limestone southern coast. One evening I met two brothers outside a cinema. I'd just watched a British film, and they'd been the only other people in the theater. When I asked whether they liked the movie, they kissed their fingers and cried,

"Beautiful! Magnifique!"

The streets, bathed in a Mediterranean sunset, were deserted, and the brothers invited me to a café, where we smoked nargile, or hookah, tobacco and drank tea for many hours.

They were Kurdish. And in Mersin, to be Kurdish was to be a foreigner in your homeland. The Kurdish People's Army, or PKK, were demanding a nation for the Kurds that included regions of Iraq, Turkey, Armenia, and Syria. Labeled as an international terrorist group, the PKK had recently detonated a bomb at a nearby naval base.

The brothers lamented their lot—they could not attend university, so during the day they sold simit, rings of sesame bread, on the street corners.

"For Kurdish, no education," said Sadik Aktas, the older brother. "For Turkish, there is education. But . . . I am Kurdish."

The brothers smashed their fists on the plastic table when, despite our best efforts, we struggled to break the barriers of language. We wrote on a scrap of notebook and used sign language to translate until we had a shared vocabulary.

"No English!" the eldest said. His frustration mirrored my own.

"No Turkish!" I replied.

Sadik and Mücahit were Sufists, and they believed in the subtlety of words. When they learned I had been to a dervish ceremony in the city of Konya, they began, first in Arabic, then in Turkish, Kurdish, and once in English, to quote the teachings of Jalluladin Rumi.

"Either exist as you are, or be as you look," they said.

We attempted to discuss literature, and when we found authors who we mutually admired, they would pronounce, kissing their fingers, "Dostoyevsky! Steinbeck! Beautiful! Magnifique!"

The brothers had a prodigious library: Whitman, Rushdie, Neruda, Mark Twain and Jack London, Tolstoy and Kafka. They wrote down for me the names of storytellers and poets they loved—Yashar Kemal, Mehmed Uzun, Nazim Hikmet, Ahmet Arif. When we parted, Sadik and Mücahit walked toward the outskirts of the city, where in the daylight I had seen the garbage and rubble piled high, noticed apartments with broken windows, and watched old men and women pushing enormous wheelbarrows piled with kindling through the dusty streets.

In Mersin, I stayed in a dive hotel. The sign in front of the building was small, barely visible. "Otel," it read. Old men sipped tea in the lobby. The faded wallpaper had peeled in places. The calendar on the wall was five years old, and the furniture was covered in sheets of stained plastic.

I had taken the luxury suite because it was the same price as a regular room and had an international TV channel. I imagined a large bed with an air conditioner but found three twin mattresses under a clattering fan. I thought the international TV station would be a news channel, but when I turned the dial on the television, pornography appeared. I assumed the room would be my own, but on my second night there I came in to find a man seated on the bed next to mine, watching a woman masturbate on the TV.

The concierge was young and liked to gripe to me about his job, though he was frustrated by our language barrier. One day, after another failed attempt at conversation, the concierge remembered that he had a friend who spoke English. The friend, however, did not live in Mersin, and I suddenly found myself on a public telephone, talking to a man who lived in a war zone. His name was Nejdet Dogan.

"You aren't in Turkey?" I asked.

"No, no, I am not Turkish, I am Kyrgyz. My country is Kyrgyzstan. You know about our civil war?"

"Yes, I know about it," I lied, thinking, where the hell is Kyrgyzstan?

"It is very bad here," he said. "I am very worried about my family. It is not safe in my city." The phone crackled, and I heard loud, explosive noises in the background.

"Where did you learn English?" I asked.

"I studied at university in Persia." The phone crackled again, staccato bursts. Later, I looked at news releases about this central Asian country I had barely heard of. People were killing each other in the city of Osh, in what the news was calling ethnic unrest. A hundred thousand people had fled their homes in the region.

Nejdet Dogan asked, "You are American?"

"I am."

"That is very good. I want to go to America, but I have no money."

"What is your job?"

"I am teacher. But now I have no job because the school . . ." He paused, a long silence. "Because the school is not there anymore."

The phone snapped with static; violent background noises continued. I felt crushed by pleasantries, my motivations for wandering trivialized by the sudden awareness of my ignorance.

"It is very hard here, my friend. My wife, now she is pregnant. But I have no job, and every day maybe the war will come to my doorway," Nejdet said.

"I understand," I told him, but of course I didn't. "But what can you do?" I asked.

"I pray. And I hope one day to leave my country. It is not a good country," he said. The crackling on the telephone grew louder. I heard shouts in the distance.

"Can we talk tomorrow? At a better time?" I asked.

"Yes, yes!" He told me. "Tomorrow is very good for me. We will talk tomorrow, God willing. Let us say four o'clock?"

"I will call you," I said.

"Insha'Allah, my friend," Nejdet said.

"Shukram, and you as well."

I hung up, thanked the desk clerk, walked up the stairs to my room, and packed my bags. I suspected suddenly that this journey was more than frivolous. It was irrational, even dangerous, and I was sure that Nejdet Dogan would not answer my call the next day. I left the hotel, pedaled to the ferry terminal, and bought a ticket for Cyprus.

Inside the ferry's cabin, a soldier in camo green smiled and offered me a cup of tea. I declined and found a seat near the television. A Turkish news agency flashed a story on the "increasing violence in Kyrgyzstan." The brief image showed a statue in a town square in the city of Osh, the face smashed by a hammer, a noose draped around the statue's neck.

←——→

I think I knew all along that my journey was a farce, that my faith didn't give me grounding in this part of the world. The belief that I could ride a bicycle wherever I wanted was absurd and only possible because of my privilege in the world. Being Orthodox didn't make this a pilgrimage. Being heartbroken didn't grant me understanding of other kinds of suffering.

The night before I boarded the ferry to Syria, I was invited to a beach party in Cyprus. We drank thick glasses of raki, anise liquor turned milky with an ice cube. Lamb kebabs and thick squares of halloumi cheese fried and sizzled on a smoky grill. Olive pits littered the sandy floorboards of the tin-roofed hut. The summer air was dry and salty and still warm. Down the beach, I could see the silhouettes of concrete bunkers and military tanks, where searchlights marked the border between the Turkish and Greek sides of the island. Out along the lapping waves, when the discordant notes of a saz player on the radio fell silent, I could hear the clattering and fluttering of crabs.

"The Kurds, they are not so bad. But the Greeks, in Greek Cyprus, I feel only hate," one of the partygoers said to me.

"But Cyprus is in the EU," I replied.

"That is a—what is the word? Hypocrite. They say Cyprus must have no border, but there is a border, and there will be no peace. Thirty-two of my family were killed in the war. The Orthodox say, 'What about our land?' but I say, 'What about my life?'" He paused. "I am Muslim, but to have no religion is better than massacre."

I wonder sometimes if perhaps the man was right. Then I think about the way in which faith can connect us to where we are, or where we once were, and to who we believe ourselves to be.

My dad once told me that he saw himself as a minority. We had been talking about prejudice, and the comment caught me by surprise. It felt, at the very least, out of touch with reality. He was talking about religion and, I suppose, speaking his truth. I think he really meant that being an Orthodox Christian in the United States made him different.

Orthodox churches aren't exactly common in the United States, and most Orthodox communities are grounded in the ethnic backgrounds of Eastern Europe. There's a vein of xenophobia running through the church, especially the church in diaspora, where faith is as much a marker of cultural identity as language, food, and family. Growing up in Orthodox in America, you learn that Catholics are wrong, that Protestants are more wrong, and that Orthodoxy is the only and original true Christian Church.

Of course, being part of a closed community does not automatically equate to persecution, or even marginalization. My father's enclave of immigrants stayed connected to their heritage not through land but through the cycle of a liturgical year. As such, the believer in me grew up certain that I could travel to the holy land, or Greece, Russia, any country that follows the Eastern Rites, and be welcomed as family. A Protestant on a pilgrimage, it was implied, is just out for a walk, but an Orthodox believer on a journey engages themselves with the deep and ancient mysteries of the one true faith.

Spiritualists and travelers share this in common: they are both envied for their fantasies. We applaud the madmen and women who flee the familiar in search of solace. Imagining I somehow earned the birthright to travel through this region by dint of my religion was an obvious delusion. But delusion among strangers felt easier than admitting the more difficult truth: that I have never been able to maintain the kind of conviction that allows my faith to thrive. Even on a Sunday morning in the church where I was raised, surrounded by family, I often feel like an outsider.

Right and wrong, Greek and Turk, good and bad. In places where history has been rewritten over and over for centuries, the constructs are gray. We do not cultivate belonging in foreign places, surrounded by someone else's muddy history. Our grappling must occur in our own communities, in the places that we are fused to by joy and pain.

←———→

My first morning in Syria, I walked to a street vendor and bought falafel, the only word in Arabic I knew with certainty. It came smothered in tahini and mayonnaise; the pita warmed through with grease. I experienced another traveler's conceit: that great food amounts to authentic experience. I rode out of Latakia believing I had done something meaningful with my time.

On the edge of town, I hit a roundabout. Four lanes of traffic spun around with no regard for the direction from which they entered, cars and motorbikes honking in an anarchic mass. I found myself crammed against a billboard of the presidential family, with Bashar al-Assad and his kids looking up toward the top of the sign, where his dead father Hafez looked down through rays of angelic light beams, a benevolent expression on his face. Car horns rose to a tempest. A transport truck brushed against my panniers.

Just then, a man shouted to me from his car window and when I turned, his wife was reaching over from the passenger seat with a cup of tea. She balanced it on a saucer.

"Welcome!" cried the man, and he pushed the teacup into my hands. As he handed me a cube of sugar, traffic began moving, and his wife shouted for her cup back. Cars brushed by, knocked me sideways, and I shuffled forward, trapped by the clumsiness of my loaded bicycle. Tea spilled and scalded my hands. The wife kept shouting; the man shouted and kept driving away. When I emerged on the highway, going south along the coast, I no longer held the teacup. Miraculously, I was still alive.

That afternoon I ate chickpeas, fresh tomatoes, and cucumbers tossed with herbs and lemon juice at an empty beach restaurant, the vegetables picked from the nearby garden. Later still, I pedaled past a collection of corrugated shacks along the beach. A young man emerged from one of the homes and shouted for me to come in. "Chai, chai," he said.

Inside, he boiled tea on a single burner balanced on a rough plank. We sat in lawn chairs and smiled at one another with the helpless looks of two people who don't speak the same language. He was from Palestine—a refugee. I asked to take his picture with my film camera, and when the negatives were developed, which wasn't until after Syria had become a war zone, I studied his face for a long time. It seemed to me that in the photo the young man's eyes blazed with animus.

Understanding the truth about my journey requires me to acknowledge and accept that I traveled at best naively, and at worst, with misogynist, imperialist, and oppressive beliefs. I was sure that by riding a bike in someone else's land, my hurt would heal. That by visiting abandoned Christian relics, I could situate my faith. I believed that through food and conversation, I could know a place. But now, when I try to recall those connections, the memories get stuck in my throat.

I cannot deny that I met friendly people. In Istanbul, the man who fixed my bike prayed for my journey, described his dreams of becoming a singer, and belted out a beautiful tenor operetta. Nearly every day, strangers shared food, stories, jokes. A farmer on the Anatolian Plateau spent ten minutes drawing a picture in the dirt depicting a trifecta of geopolitical terror—the United States, the United Kingdom, and Israel—then tore a pea plant from his garden by the roots and sent me off with fresh veggies for my lunch.

I followed the Syrian coast south and into Lebanon for a few days. In Lebanon, I was welcomed into a monastery by a nun. The only words we shared were in Slavonic, and we had afternoon tea while shouting "Christ is Risen!" to one another. A woman in Tripoli taught me to make soap. Everywhere I rode, people chased down my bicycle with offers of tea. The kindness overwhelmed me. Said a man one afternoon, "If you go to hell, I think you will find friendly people there."

Years of reflection have left me certain that I failed to comprehend the anger of the region. Even after poring through my words and memories for clues, I still can't say why I went in the first place—pilgrimage, heartbreak, dumb American on vacation? Maybe the reason I went doesn't matter as much as the impact of the journey. Those images of war, so incongruous with my experience, don't feel real. Even now, so many years later, they leave me unhinged. Of the adventures I have undertaken since, the farthest from home I have been bold enough to venture is Canada.

In Beirut I attended Divine Liturgy at the Greek Orthodox cathedral and afterward, took a bus out to the city museum. Tucked in among eight thousand years of civilization—Egyptians, Phoenicians, Assyrians, Romans, Crusaders, Ottomans—I came across a glass case holding what looked like a carcinogenic mass. Hunks of silver had fused with charred terracotta and flecked with drippings of mucus-green glass. The card near it explained: "The terrible condition of these objects as well as the fusion of metal, ivory, glass, and stone are the result of high temperatures reached during a fire caused by the shelling of a storage area."

In front of that display case, I began to cry. How trivial my own issues seemed. How wrong my self-righteousness, to imagine that I, a foreigner, understood the feelings of strangers. Today, even the youngest children know explosions and stray bullets and soldiers and the stain of blood. Today, I still feel a great weight of shame.

At the gate to the Old City of Damascus, a turbaned sheik smoked a cigarette below a statue of Salahaddin slaying an infidel. Nearby, the Barada River, which has kept Damascus alive for more than eight thousand years, trickled over the worn stones of an archeological dig; plastic bottles rode by on the riffles.

Few places allow the traveler to forget the familiar and act out their Arabian Nights fantasies like Damascus. In the stone alleys near the Umayyad Mosque, sellers crouched over wares spread out on carpets in front of them. Men hung ancient lanterns over the arches leading back to spice stands mounded high with cumin and cardamom, Hungarian paprika and Eritrean salt. The bazaar was a maze, with stands of Turkish delight, pistachios, and raw goat meat; aisles of colorful scarves and gauzy cloth; stalls of fake sunglasses and used cell phones. I passed robed Saudi tourists and Palestinians with checkered turbans, women who veiled even their eyes and men in fezzes who carried backpacks dispensing black tea. I fingered carpets from Armenia, Turkey, Iran, Pakistan, and China. I walked into shops full of tarnished lamps, shops of gold and silver, pipe shops, coffee shops, tea shops, leather shops, furniture shops, pillow shops, suit shops, and shops that sold lingerie with bangles hanging from the lacy brassieres and red leather thongs. "Some cities oust or smother their past," writes Colin Thubron, "Damascus lives in hers."

Along the carpet seller's street, I met the art dealer Ahmet, whose tiny shop was dug into the wall like a catacomb. He had hundreds of variations on the same stereotypes: veiled women with saccharine eyes; silhouetted camel caravans under a single star; minarets jabbing up through the haze of an oasis.

"Painting is like a first love," said Ahmet. "You think it is everything, but when it gets stale, it is no good. You must learn new techniques, change your eye, and it will be like real love, like a real painting."

He flipped through the stacks and pulled out two paintings of alleyways in the Christian Quarter.

"Fawaz al-Bibi. He is the best. I talk all the time with Fawaz al-Bibi. I say, why do you not paint the mosque or the dervish? He will not paint the mosques. He said it is not good for him. Al-Bibi is Druze, and so—no mosque!"

I had never heard of Druze, knew nothing of their beliefs, but these paintings were different.

The gray and brown hues in the work of Fawaz al-Bibi were applied with knife and brush. He had created shadows where there should be light, light where I expected shadow. I know little of art, but his brick archways, his teetering balconies, and the phantom figures, who appeared only through the vaguest silhouettes, floated away from the painting, descending deeper into those mysterious alleys of the artist's Damascus. Al-Bibi seemed to me an artist who understood the duality of his people. Somewhere in those paintings, I wondered if I might find a path for my own redemption.

←——————→

I have since read that most Damascene artists have left Syria. A few have found galleries in cities like Dubai, Beirut, and Toronto to show their work. Some have started new projects—they stretch military uniforms for canvas and paint images of guns, cemetery crosses, gray tones of an old city wall ripped through with crimson. The exiles paint in proxy studios, their work furious and immediate, artistic acts of protest or catharsis.

I bought the two paintings. After the trip, I hung them over my writing desk back home. Sometimes I still get lost in them: I pretend that the paintings contain the pain of a now-ruined city, that they will teach me what has been lost in the war. I conjure a memory just outside the streets painted in the frames.

In this memory, I am pedaling along the coast, just north of the Lebanon border, and I see a sign in English that reads "Phoenician Ruins." I follow the road past greenhouses filled with tomatoes and cucumbers, spin up a hill to a gravel parking lot with a sign in Arabic. I am alone. Enormous burial towers jut up from the field, pink sandstone pockmarked by millennia of salt breeze.

I leave my bicycle to find an angle for a photograph. The Mediterranean Sea swirls against the cliffs a kilometer away, and I can just hear the surf as I step around the thorny plants that have fractured the temple foundation. My hand runs across the flesh of an ancient pillar. Suddenly camouflage netting stretches toward me, spilling from the excavated ruins of Marathos. Hidden under the mesh are a half dozen surface-to-air missiles. It is like a bad action movie. I tuck my camera under my shirt and back down the hill slowly. When I reach the highway, I pedal for fifty kilometers. I do not stop.

←——————→

I remember those missiles as a scene disconnected from most of the journey. My photographs depict tea sellers and children, families on aged carpets and men leaning against old cars or over rows of ancient lamps—images that fit with what I had expected, pictures of the exotic. But now, looking back, I want to know what I missed. I want to know how to grieve.

In Damascus, I spent a morning near the Grand Bazaar's spice alley, in a small *souq* filled with perfumists. A young man at the al-Ghabra perfume shop called me over.

Vials of essential oils lined the shelves: white musk, lavender, gardenia, vanilla, citrus, and jasmine. "The oils come from Paris. I mix them. Or I buy the mix and add the alcohol," said Anas, the shopkeeper.

With a glass syringe Anas extracted a few milliliters of essence and injected it into an ornate bottle. With another syringe, he added alcohol. He swirled the mixture once, twice, three times. He added three drops of sandalwood extract.

"The fixative," he said.

He said he could teach me to mix perfumes if I would help him with English idioms. I spent two hours at the stand. I made him a list—kick the bucket, mad as a hornet, bite the dust, the last straw.

He taught me which essences, notes, pair well together. Rosemary balances geranium; artemisia complements patchouli. I learned how to blend the fixative to make the scents last longer. That seemed the important part: getting the power of these smells to linger after the wearer had gone.

In the Orthodox tradition, Holy Friday concludes with a vesperal service where Christ's body is taken from the cross and placed in the tomb. The *plashchanitsa*, a life-size cloth icon depicting Christ in his funereal shroud, is transported from the altar to the center of the church. The ceremony of this movement contains the first hint of the coming Resurrection. It is perhaps my favorite service.

Before Christ is laid to rest in front of the congregation, the priest and altar servers circle the church's interior with the shroud of Christ. In the memories of my youth, the old women cried, people bowed before the icon, and kissed the icon's feet. The recollection of the choir singing the troparion during the procession still brings a lump to my throat. Holy Friday is a day of deep mourning, but something in the hymn sung at the end of that service, in the bell-clank of the censer, the thick incense smoke, and the music lifting toward heaven, alludes to the coming joy.

The perfume conjured for me a similar moment of longing, as if the right blend could recover something lost—my faith, my relationship, my sense of belonging. But I was, once again, wrong. About two years after I moved to Alaska, I knocked the bottle onto my dry cabin floor, where it shattered. For a few days my home reeked, the scent so sweet it nearly choked me. Eventually it faded, then disappeared.

←——→

I met my friend Bassam next to the statue of Salahaddin outside the citadel. We hadn't seen each other in several years—since college, where he had been the host of an annual spring party dubbed "Bassam-a-palooza," which had included a bluegrass band and several kegs of beer.

"Merhaba," he cried, and swallowed me in a bear hug.

We caught up on the latest college gossip at a café near the Christian Quarter that dated back over five hundred years to the

Mamluk Era. It was warm out and we wandered from square to square, eating sweet desserts and street food and smoking nargile. We laughed at old memories, but lost in the magic of Damascus, it felt strange to recall clichéd college experiences.

"I think I could probably just live here for a while," said Bassam. "Teach English, smoke hookahs, relax."

Bassam's cousins were building a weekend home on the edge of the city, and the next evening his cousin Fatih drove us out to the half-finished house to watch a World Cup match and to swim in the newly finished swimming pool. We talked construction: plumbing, electricity, finish carpentry. Fatih thought the work would be done before winter.

"We have the pool ready first—that is the most important," said Fatih. We swam, and I reveled in the normalcy of it all.

$$\longleftarrow\longrightarrow$$

One afternoon, Bassam and I took a bus to Homs so we could visit a Crusader castle. Crac du Chevalier had been built on a high mountaintop and had once held two thousand people, plus chickens, goats, horses, manure, chamber pots, bad food, diphtherial water, and not a single bathtub.

"A thousand years and it still smells disgusting," Bassam said.

Crac du Chevalier was built to hold back Salahaddin's army, but in the end, it couldn't stave off the homesickness of the Crusaders who built it. They left the moats and caverns, the cathedral and guard towers and walls to crumble with time. But a fortress this formidable doesn't fall easily. When we came into a courtyard where staircases climbed and descended like an Escher painting, I thought that with a little work, the place could be livable again soon.

For Bassam and me, the castle brought back the fantastic dreams of childhood. We played Robin Hood and King Richard and fought great battles along looming passages.

"Die infidel!" Bassam shouted.

"Perish, heathen," I yelled. A group of Chinese tourists saw us jousting with our imaginary swords and asked to take our picture. We quit playing and moved on. Three years later, in 2013, the government and rebel forces would fight for control of this ancient fortress. More than two dozen people would be killed.

That night we went to the hills above Damascus to see the city at night. We smoked nargile and ate plates of pita, hummus, tomatoes, and cucumbers. Fatih laughed at us while we again told stories from college, when we'd once head-butted each other at a party, and had, another time, been thrown out of a bar on a Sunday morning.

"Sometimes I am glad I do not live in America. I think it is too intense for me," said Fatih.

$$\longleftrightarrow$$

There are three Christian villages in the hills above Damascus—Jabadeen, Sarka, and Maalula—and these three towns still speak Aramaic, the language of Christ. I left my bicycle at the hotel, took a bus to Maalula for the afternoon, and visited the monastery of St. Thecla.

The day was calm, warm. The landscape around Maalula seemed imbued with balance. At the monastery, I paid a nun for a candle, and she led me into the chapel. I recited a prayer—more from habit than communion—lit my candle, and left the damp of the nave. I wandered through the cleft in the rock where St. Thecla was said to have escaped from the Romans and ate lunch at a restaurant where two other tourists argued about the use of Aramaic in a Mel Gibson movie.

I found myself wondering what had drawn me to this holy site at all. I didn't even know much about St. Thecla. She was an early disciple who traveled with St. Paul. She had fended off violent acts in her youth, narrowly escaped martyrdom several times, and used a nearby cleft in these mountains to escape Roman troops. She died of old age, blessed by God.

I imagined myself to be traveling through the Holy Land, but mostly I had encountered dry countryside. I wanted to envision my journey as a pilgrimage, but it was beginning to feel more like avoidance. Pilgrimages usually have clear destinations—Mecca, Jerusalem, the holy relics of a saint. Even when the journey is metaphorical, pilgrims generally know what they are looking for.

I was searching for a Christianity that only existed in the imaginations of people who still wouldn't admit that Constantinople had fallen. In the real world, government forces would shell the town and kill twenty-five civilians less than two years later. Rebels would kidnap the nuns from the monastery and hold them for ransom along the Iraq border. When fighting ended, out of thirty-three hundred residents, only fifty would remain in Maalula.

"Whoever does not believe will not live but will die forever," said St. Thecla to a magistrate before he ordered her burned. I ache with the impotence of language.

←——→

The semifinals of the World Cup were played between Germany and Spain while I was in Damascus, and someone at my hotel secured an invitation to watch the match at the German embassy. The Germans were so excited about the game that I wasn't even asked for identification when I entered the compound. Everywhere, people drank thick beers and ate sausages dipped in bowls of mustard. In the space of a taxi ride, I had departed the Levant for a biergarten in Munich.

I met a woman named Cate at the party. Cate, a Canadian, had hopped buses up from Cairo.

"Did you get butterflies in your stomach before you came to the Middle East?" she asked. Before I could answer, she said, "I got them. I hadn't gotten them from traveling in a long time. God, it was a good feeling."

I asked her, "Why Syria?" It was the same question I would be asked by customs agents on my flight home.

"People ask me what I'm running from all the time," Cate said. "But I'm not running. I just can't explain why I love this life."

Spain scored a goal, and the German diplomats groaned. An emissary wife came around with chocolate-and-cherry tarts—a family recipe. I poured myself another beer. Outside on the street, cars and motorbikes circled the embassy, cheering, taunting, honking, and waving flags.

"I think it can be a tough life. We're scrutinized for it. The grass is always greener, you know?" I said.

"No," she said. "I think we need people who are content with having ordinary lives. Otherwise, we'd probably drift off the earth. My best friend is like that. I used to pity her lifestyle, but she calls me out . . . she just really wanted to have a family and a husband. I'd be lost and jaded without her."

"Yeah," I said, and that explorer in my head, the one searching the edges of the map, shriveled.

I was a tourist, a pseudo-spiritualist pedaling through a hookah haze of self-deception. The Syria I was visiting would become a checkmark on the world atlas, one more story to recite as proof of my eccentricity. Meanwhile, where I had played games in the hallways of Crac du Chevalier, dead bodies would be left to rot.

I called my ex-girlfriend that evening from my hotel. I asked for another chance. I painted rose-colored visions of possible futures, of reconciliation. She hedged but eventually agreed to give our relationship one more chance.

I think I knew even then that the relationship had ended. In two months, we would break up for good. I would feel the pain of that final split with less uncertainty than I would watching Syria's descent into chaos from afar, as a stranger who had deluded himself into thinking he understood.

It would be years before I allowed myself to be vulnerable enough to admit that I had been angry at her. It would be just as long before I admitted my culpability in hiding that anger behind a veneer of rationalism and bluster. And it would be even longer before I realized that the anger stemmed from guilt, in part because I never tried to see her for who she was. Instead of complexity, I'd seen archetype. I wanted desperately to be heard, but it never occurred to me that I had also needed to listen.

When I was a kid, obsessed with fishing, I knew the fish would spook if I didn't strive for silence. I watched my elders—Mr. Radevich, my grandmother, my father—standing in the back of the church in silent observation. I wonder now how much of religion, for them, was really about the teachings. Maybe, just maybe, faith in God isn't so much about truth as about paying attention.

My journal is filled with pages upon pages of images I believed held deeper meaning, but which now seem empty. I was a man whose self-concept was implacable, traveling within the tunnel vision of my privilege. Why has it taken me so long to realize that neither faith nor love contain certainty, that they are only possible if I'm willing to shut up?

←——————→

Maybe it came from the light, inextricable from the alleys and desert, but I think what made Syria seem so filled with ancient magic stemmed from mystery—that is, mystery at its origin, where it means mastery, initiation, and mistress. In Western culture, we haven't retained the complex tenets of the mysterious, but in a world of souqs and mosques, scented with jasmine and incense, where Druze and Muslim and Christian pray in labyrinthine streets, I could still believe that mysticism remained. Clerics lounge in olivewood doorways; booksellers tender copies of the Koran gilded with gold; dried chickpeas and glass beads roll down onto the stones built upon stones built upon cities that stretch back to an era when even language was in its infancy. The high-rises, the cell phones, cars, and light bulbs all vibrate against the colossal wave of civilization begun here untold millennia ago. The world grows outward from Damascus.

I left the city at night, by bus. I took the wheels off my bicycle, loaded it into the luggage compartment, and slept all the way to the Turkish border. I carried with me typical trinkets—a nargile pipe, a gilded Byzantine icon, the paintings by Fawaz-al Bibi.

Maybe I could have paid more attention: to the billboards of Bashir al-Assad looking to the heavens for help from his dead father, to the Palestinian boy offering tea, to Fatih when I mentioned world politics.

"We have to be careful with our conversation," he said, and glanced around while he stoked coals in the nargile.

Probably we learn the same thing from opening our eyes to the unfamiliar as we learn from the prayers we offer on a pilgrimage. Had I looked closer, I might have crawled to the tip of the forged steel blade and witnessed a region on the brink of collapse. I might have realized the difference between literary hüzün and earnest rage. Had I looked closer, it wouldn't have made a damn bit of difference.

I bicycled the desert adrift in my own ephemeral problems. Now that bombs have destroyed so much, I can't even recall enough of the places where I wandered to know what to lament

The traveler's conceit as pathetic façade: I replaced reality with a stereotype of the Middle East. I saw dervishes and djinns where there were soldiers and rebels, imagined harems and hamams instead of insurrections. The camels, the streets scented with myrrh, and the muezzin's call to prayer didn't embody a knowledge of this place any more than the funny hats and strange chants of Orthodox priests reveal my relationship with God.

Since my visit, more than eleven million people—Syrians, Kurds, even Turks—have been displaced from their homes. Almost five hundred thousand more are dead. Like the rest of the world, I've learned to ignore the news footage, the rubble-strewn streets, and the millions of people pressing against violence that has drawn on now for more than a decade. My memories, so vivid with the magic of the Orient, have been supplanted by the convolutions of a war waged in the name of too many ideologies.

I no longer believe in some collective nostalgia. I spent the long hours on my bicycle lamenting my failed relationship back home, searching for something familiar to appease my own selfish spirituality. I might have cried for the land instead. I might have wondered: must a civilization go to war to know the difference between pleasure and fear? I might have just stayed home.

←——————→

That feeling—the pride that comes when a traveler believes they have acquired a knowledge not theirs to possess—is gone. I rifle through my memories, and the same scene appears, again and again. It has clarified with time.

I see a boy, just learning to walk. His family crouches near the wall of the Umayyad Mosque with a basket of food. Hundreds of Syrian flags hang overhead, fluttering on taut wires. The family is having a picnic. While the mother serves lunch, the child toddles into a flock of pigeons. The birds squawk, rise, settle. They want the food in the basket. The boy giggles, charges at them, retreats, charges again. At last, the father scoops the child and the family leaves. The pigeons loiter for a minute and then, in a sweep of wings, rise above the bazaar and depart.

Of Big Burns and Ghost Towns

The life of fire comes from the death of earth. The life of air comes from the death of fire. The life of water comes from the death of air. The life of earth comes from the death of water.

Fire, in time, catches up with everything.

—HERACLITUS OF EPHESUS

*U*NTIL I WAS ordered to weigh our gear for the helicopter ride, I had never even heard of Flat, Alaska.

"I think we're getting sent to Flat," my boss said while we waited for work orders at the Alaska Division of Forestry fire base in McGrath. He spoke as if I was supposed to know where Flat was, and why it was important. My boss often spoke this way—assuming I knew what he was talking about—regardless of whether I had context to understand him.

Maybe he thought I knew so much because for me, fighting fire was just a summer job to pay for graduate school. I think that's how I got the nickname "Professor."

"Hey, Professor," guys would ask, "what kind of bird is that?"

"Hey, Professor, is it rainy in Costa Rica in November?"

It didn't matter that I studied English and not biology or geography, and besides, it was better than the season I had worked in Arizona, when, because I have a lazy eye, I'd ended up with the nickname "Crazy Eyes."

Between 2008 and 2013, I spent three seasons working as a wildland firefighter, first in Arizona on a Hotshot crew and later in Alaska on a Type 2 Initial Attack crew that functioned pretty much like a Hotshot crew with an inferiority complex. I still feel those seasons in my blood. I miss the endless miles of tussock swamp, the bar oil in my hair, the sweet stench of smoldering black spruce on a subarctic morning. The seasons I spent fighting fire were, for me, the most meaningful and enjoyable periods of my working life.

Yet I hold a deep antipathy toward life on a fire crew. In fire I found a culture chock-full of misogyny, machismo, and prejudice. The status quo was male, tough, detached, and white. Anything different got belittled. My former saw partner Ben Meyer, one of only a few people I have stayed in touch with from those years, once described the posturing on a fire crew in crude terms: "Imagine that you're always carrying a measuring tape in your pocket, just in case you need to pull your dick out and let everyone know that yours is bigger."

In a job where chauvinism is part of an identity, it starts to feel abnormal to meet somebody who isn't an asshole. You spend two weeks, sometimes three, on your feet for sixteen hours a day, walking hillsides, not showering, eating military rations for food, with a film of ash, sweat, and tobacco spit accumulating on your clothes and body, and the sexist commentary from the guy in front of you becomes almost endearing. You ignore the social problems because the work is hard. Because even on a slow day, you can never forget that the work is dangerous, that burned trees can fall on you, that you can stick your boot in liquid ash and broil your leg, that fire can kill you.

I have no wish to return to the fire line, to the long hours for bad pay, the weeks of filth and heavy packs and walk-the-line hierarchy, but I miss the almost mythical feeling of it. On that morning in McGrath, when the helicopter lifted off, I thought to myself, I have entered a fable, and I get to be the hero. The rotors snapped us across the Kuskokwim Basin, spinning toward the old ghost town, and I almost believed it was possible.

My hardest day of firefighting came on a burn operation during a Northern California night shift in late August of my rookie year. Every morning, the sun pulled shadows from the mountains, and the fire complex we'd been assigned to blew over roads and torched huge stands of pine and fir. In daytime, the inferno grew so large it developed its own weather patterns. A hundred thousand acres had already burned, and two firefighters had died—one killed in a helicopter, another by a falling tree.

We worked when the humidity rose with the dark. On this evening we'd already been on the clock for ten hours of the day shift, swinging into the red-eyed night without sleep. Our bosses decided to attempt an operation that relied on holding the fire along a narrow road midway down a mountain slope. It was a risky strategy, and we faced several watch-out situations already— working a mid-slope line, working at night in new country, working in California. But politicians and the public were getting nervous, so we climbed from our vehicles and buckled on our packs for the night ahead.

Success in a burn operation relies on a deep knowledge of how fires usually behave. You need to know that fire attracts fire, that fire runs uphill. You need to understand how flames react to specific humidity, wind speed, air temperature, fuel type. You need people to watch the fire from afar, to monitor micro-changes in weather almost every minute, to have an escape route, a safety zone, an army of firefighters guarding against sparks that would ignite on the wrong side of the line. You need shared radio frequencies, air support, intimate topographic knowledge. Everyone and everything must work in perfect synchrony. The margins for error are slim.

Chainsaws spit grease and dust into the darkness; another crew was called in for extra support, and we kept only tenuous control on the fire. My assignment paired me with my friend Wade Tait; we were tasked with igniting a line of brush upslope of the road. In theory, if we put just the right amount of heat on the ground, we would create a second fire that pulled into the main flame front, containing the blaze in a wall of ash and dead trees.

Wade and I took up our drip torches and double-checked the gas ratios—75 percent diesel, 25 percent gasoline, so the mix didn't leap across the dry air and burn through our Nomex yellows and greens when the canisters drizzled flame—and went to work.

Within a minute, flames licked the lower branches of trees. Towering ponderosa exploded, spitting fire two hundred feet into the air. Just then an order came over the radio to stop working.

"The Type 2 crew came. They just drove their bus off the road," the radio crackled.

A long pause came, and the fire we lit moved uphill, the roar fading as it reached the mountaintop. The bosses called in a crane to lift the bus back onto the road. When orders came to start moving again, we needed to move fast. Our torches flung flame along the ground, and I stumbled to keep pace. Every now and then, Wade would call out some encouragement. Just a few words—"Good spacing" or "Nice work, Messick." It was enough to keep me going.

My world blurred to red haze and adrenaline. We poured fire and we moved, hacking through thick manzanita and scrub oak, falling, singeing our hair, tearing our clothes, scraping across the steep slope while blasts of heat seared us from behind.

Once, I got tangled in a piece of burning brush. I fought back panic as I struggled to break loose from the branches. When I scrambled free, Wade walked up and calmly slapped out the flames climbing up my pant leg.

The fire line held, the fiery night turned into an ashen dawn. We tied our burn into another section of the fire. Our work for that day finished, Wade sat down beside me and shook burned leaves from his clothes.

His beard was flecked and burned. His shirt was grotesque, torn and starchy from weeks of sweat and ash. He had a cut on one cheek, his eyes were hollow, his belt notched as tight as it could go—he'd cut new holes into it with his pocketknife.

We didn't high-five, and Wade didn't have some smart-ass comment about being tough. We just sat there, tired.

You build bonds fast on a fire crew—it's almost compulsive, this bonding and othering, the formation of a group identity that borders on the erotic.

At the end of my first week as a rookie, after long days of pack hikes and endless training sessions, we sat on the front porch of the barracks, looking out at the sunset across the pinyon pine flats with beers in our hands, and fought each other.

A guy we called "Big Tony" was trying to convince rookies to wrestle, and Big Tony decided he wanted to see me fight Wade Tait. Wade was tall and gangly—he had long hair and a beard that earned him the nickname "Baby Jesus." After the fire season, Wade and I would take bicycles down to Mexico and ride from the Yucatan Peninsula down to Panama. The following summer, we would paddle more than a thousand miles through the Canadian Arctic. But I remember on that night wanting so badly to win the fight, to be accepted by this strange fraternity, that I didn't hesitate. I dove for Wade's legs with all the skill of a guy who wrestled half a season in high school.

Wade, calm as could be, slipped me into a half nelson and pinned me to the hardwood deck. It took less than fifteen seconds for him to kick my ass.

"Fuckin' squirrel strength," someone said, and Big Tony handed us each another beer.

When you share your strength and tenacity with twenty other people, and are always ready to prove that strength, a mob mentality develops. Ninety-nine percent of the time, this coping mechanism works because the inflated self-esteem and the misanthropy are necessary in order to, after sixteen hours of trailing your hands through cold ash, shrug your shoulders and leap back into the fray to catch a spot fire. Ninety-nine percent of the time, you write it down as overtime, proof that you are good at your job.

It's much too easy to forget that in fighting fire, you face off against the most powerful and dangerous force on earth, and nothing will save you if you get it wrong. In the first two years of this work, I clung to that mob mentality and machismo like a talisman, believing it would protect me.

Not until we were sent to save the ghost town of Flat, on a different crew and several years later, did I begin to see cracks in the façade that holds fire culture together. I'd worked nearly three seasons, responding to bellowed commands like an automaton, walking in lines, trying to prove my strength. Even then, it took a national tragedy for me to question whether hegemony and toughness were enough to keep me alive. Even now, years later, I'm still not sure what the answer might be.

When I moved to Alaska and joined a crew there, I asked to be put on a chainsaw. Even though it meant lugging around an extra thirty pounds of gear, I wanted to be on saw because when the engine revved to 14,000 rpms, you couldn't hear people talk.

Running a chainsaw on a fire crew is a team effort—it includes sawyer and swamper. The sawyer carries the saw, and the swamper carries the gas and bar oil. A saw team does everything together except sleep and go to the bathroom. You cut tank for tank. You share responsibility for keeping the saw clean, the teeth sharp, and the gas mixed for the next day's work. Your life revolves around the saw.

That's how I met Ben Meyer. Ben was the kind of person who, on day twelve of a hard roll when you think you can't work for even another hour and your feet feel like hamburger and all you want is a shower, would turn off the saw and ask if you had heard anything recently about what Mary Kate and Ashley Olsen were up to.

We bonded over shared penchants for banjo ballads, obscure art, and quirky literature. The crew referred to us as "the professor and the scientist"; it wasn't really meant as a compliment. We both struggled to fit in with the crew's culture. Like me, Ben didn't quite trust the face value of our roles.

Ben helped me understand that part of the draw of fighting fire comes from learning to live comfortably with nature at its most powerful and destructive. He reminded me how lucky we were to walk through some of the most remote forest on the continent, to fly into some of the most beautiful and strange landscapes I have ever seen. Ben reminded me that I fought fire not just because I loved the paychecks but because I loved wilderness.

Two years after we both quit fire, Ben wrote me a letter from Nepal. He had just completed a ten-day silent meditation retreat and was traveling around Katmandu with an expatriate clown named Ron. The letter was thirty-one pages long and outlined an allegorical novel he wanted to write about some of his experience on fire crews. To capture the allegory, he wrote, "One of the characters needed to be psychologically scarred by a monomaniacal sociopath because he does not fulfill the vision of a devoted tribe member."

In Ben's synopsis, a military veteran struggling with PTSD starts finding hundred-dollar bills littered through the woods behind the Fairbanks dry cabin he has just moved into. Upon inspection, he discovers that his outhouse is a part of a network of magical portals, and because the man wants to make the world a better place, he decides to use his outhouse portal to send Christmas presents to needy children around the world.

But his effort to spread the magic of Christmas starts to corrupt the man—his ego grows with each gift delivered, and he comes to believe himself to actually be Santa Claus (actually be a hero). He starts hiring seasonal labor to help him with his cause. These young, optimistic workers, or elves (rookies on a fire crew), are idealistic, seduced by Santa's "charisma and charm." As the organization grows and time passes, the teleportal gift operation gets subsumed by greed. Santa's elves find themselves jumping into shitholes to help multinational companies evade millions of dollars in corporate taxes, all in the name of the holiday spirit.

One of these "elves" isn't so sure about all this. His coworkers appear to have bought in to the culture of Santa's workshop and take enormous pride in their work. Yet something about Santa's system seems very off. "The boy's motivations to work as an elf were originally wholesome and genuine, but as he grows disillusioned with finding out what elves really do . . . he becomes mean-spirited, and he snaps," Ben wrote.

Perplexing as the plot was, I felt it described perfectly the sense of inadequacy that grows out of fire's toe-the-line culture of machismo. Ben's question to me was this: "If firefighters were elves in Santa's workshop, what would be the equivalent of carrying the cubee?"

Some context for the uninitiated: The cubee is the most important tool on a fire and the bane of every rookie's existence. You carry other important equipment—fire shelter, extra chains for the chainsaw, headlamps, files, eye protection, food, lengths of rope, batteries for your radio—but the cubee is the real lifeline for firefighters. It contains the water we drink.

The name comes from their shape, five-gallon bladders of water dropped into a cardboard box and wrapped with fiber tape to give it support. They are usually threaded through a tool handle and carried like a hobo rucksack. It digs into your shoulder like a fist. Few things will break a person faster than carrying a cubee to the top of a mountain.

In Arizona, beating back flames in one-hundred-degree heat, it was standard protocol for each person to drink a gallon of water per hour. In Alaska, where we relied on helicopters and riverboats and fought fire in tussock swamps, our crew emptied five or more cubees during a workday. It is a point of both pride and agony for a rookie to carry the cubee. I've seen crew members come nearly to blows in their efforts to haul the extra forty pounds of water up a steep hill.

In his letter, Ben described the catalyst for his novel, from his rookie season as a hotshot, and it felt hauntingly familiar. The hurry up and wait, the way your effort to prove your physical ability or demonstrate an understanding of firefighting tactics was either ignored or belittled. The pressure to be tough, indifferent to pain, to be better than both fellow crew members and the land itself. The ferocious sense of competition that thrives on making those who don't fit in feel small.

Ben's crew had been working late-season fires in the Lower 48 and found themselves stuck "at a Best Western in Fresno watching cartoons and eating pizza and trying on cowboy boots at the Mexican mall across the street while waiting on vehicle repairs." When they returned to work, they were assigned to an Idaho fire at six thousand feet and tasked with holding a rocky ridgetop. Ben wrote:

We were jolted back to reality after our indolent detour. For four or five days in a row we began our mornings with a two-hour hike up to the ridge, gaining several thousand feet en route. Each of these mornings, like all mornings, was an opportunity to get the cubee.

. . . Get the cubee. Get the cubee. Each morning that passed in which I did not get the cubee, my inadequacy grew. And then one morning, I got the cubee. We hiked. The steepest part came in the first 45 minutes. Nearly burst a lung. I saw spots. I should have just kept chasing the spots, should have kept carrying the fucker, but instead at the next water break, after 45 minutes or so of hiking uphill, I passed the cubee off to Swanson behind me. Fuck. Also, God bless him.

It must have been just after Swanson had the box situated over his shoulder that [the squad boss] in front glanced back to assess line order. He, with whom I had exchanged about a dozen words since May, including being gifted these observations: "On a lesser crew, you'd be solidly in the middle of the pack," and "I guess you help out a lot with camp chores," saw that indeed it was Swanson who had hoisted the cubee that day and not me.

Ben tried to redeem himself in the eyes of the crew leaders the next day. He described a tooth-and-nail wrestling match to again get a cubee for the morning hike, only to have the water bag break open and soak him through. He found himself further ostracized,

left grinning like an idiot with superfluous, leaking cargo, able to do nothing but laugh at the whole ritual. It was at this moment that [the crew boss] must have glanced back to see what the hold-up was.

And so I hiked cubee-less that day. In the next two mornings, McCormick and then Sanchez didn't give up their cubees at the same water break spot where I had given up mine the day before, because they are strong and I am weak. When we arrived at our destination two hours and several thousand feet higher in elevation later, I was called upon by [the crew boss] for a private discussion. Between intervals of chew-spit he tells me he thinks I owe the crew an apology for what happened this morning.

I search for a moment before I realize he's talking about the leaking cubee. I'm not sure what to apologize for. "It looked like you were pretty happy once you realized you didn't have to carry it. You haven't carried the cubee since . . . when? I turn around and see you with a big shit-eating grin with a leaker and just looked fucked up. So I think you owe everyone an apology for your attitude."

I didn't say anything. He spit again and told me to go back to work.

I remember falling asleep that night with my fists still clenched, not bothering to take off my boots or crawl in the sleeping bag, the mantra "shit-eating grin" lodged somewhere in the mucus of my sinuses. For the next 24 hours, I experienced a physical paroxysm of anger unlike anything before or since. Every miscommunication and failure I'd endured the whole summer was melted into a branding iron stamped on my frontal lobes.

$$\longleftarrow \longrightarrow$$

During your first years in fire, you get taught not to think too much. Keep your head on a swivel, be adaptable, stay alert, speak up—but also, keep your head down, don't ask too many questions, how you feel doesn't matter, just do your job. The apparent conflict between these behavioral lessons makes it often feel impossible to get it right. But the dichotomy is essential—these lessons keep you alive.

Our society holds firefighters up as heroes—anyone who risks themselves to save lives and property is beyond reproach. During fire season, you walk into a gas station in your filthy clothes, and people thank you for keeping them safe. They shake your hand and buy you coffee while you stand at the checkout. You smile and nod but really you just want to buy another can of Copenhagen.

The best firefighters I know accept this public outpouring of support with a sardonic gruffness. If they have been in long enough, they know somebody who died on a fire. None of my crew bosses were easy people to deal with—they were distant, close-minded, often mean—but they saw their job, first and foremost, as protecting the lives and safety of their crew. Most of them did it well.

What hit so hard about Ben's cubee story was how commonplace it felt. That sense of living under constant scrutiny—the kind of totalitarian oversight that leaves no room for privacy and eats away at a person's nerves—often feels like a fire crew's status quo. For rookies especially, the job interview never really ends, and the inevitable mistakes, however small, rarely get a nuanced examination that might allow someone to really learn from them. I never quite understood, when so much of fire behavior balances on a razor edge, why the most constructive criticism I ever received in my rookie season basically amounted to "don't fuck up."

I think only once did I ever feel the palpable risk of the work. Ben and I had been asked by a squad boss, an assistant leader, to search for spot fires along a stretch of smoldering fire line. All that day, nothing had sparked. No trees were torching, the wind was light. It was a good day to secure a corner of the fire. Most of the crew worked cutting brush and digging back any burnable material from the simmering edge. Ben and I were the only two patrolling the green side for lingering spots. We climbed through thick stands of black spruce that nearly choked us. It was slow and taxing work. We kept our eyes and noses open for smells or signs of anything burning. Fire can be good at staying hidden, so we stayed diligent.

By accident, someone on the fire line not forty yards from us tossed a burnt stick onto the unburned pile of brush that had been pulled away from the fire edge. At that same moment, the sun popped from behind a cloud and a gust of wind came up. Within a few seconds, the brush transformed from an inert pile of sticks into a moving inferno. It ripped into the black spruce stand where we were patrolling and formed a forty-foot wall of flame that stretched for fifty yards. Neither Ben nor I had a radio. Ben fired up his chainsaw, I plastered myself to his side, slinging away the cut branches, and we worked like madmen to claw our way back into the black. The fire burned through where we had been standing in less than two minutes. Once we reached safety, we retreated with the rest of the crew back down the line.

Our quick thinking and fast reaction kept us from deploying a fire shelter. We explained what had happened. Our boss stopped work, called the crew together, and for a half hour discussed every single detail of what went wrong with communication in the incident. He demanded a plan to avoid future failures. At the end of the workday, to remind us how mild errors have grave consequences, everyone did pushups until we collapsed.

In truth, work on fire is often tedious. There is a lot of hurry up and wait, hours standing around while plans of attack are coordinated, and afterward, waiting at a makeshift helicopter pad for a ride back to base camp. I remember once we grew so bored waiting that we convinced a guy to eat an entire jar of mayonnaise. He didn't even do it for money.

Probably more than three-quarters of a crew's work on a wildfire is "mopping up." This requires a slow walk through cold, blackened trees looking for residual heat that could creep out of the burn area and reignite the living forest nearby. In a sixteen-hour shift, a crew might cover less than a thousand feet of the fire's edge, digging in smoldering duff and spraying with water that they generally haul around on their backs. The success of mop-up depends on an extended game of telephone, passing messages up and down an evenly spaced line of people, bent over with heavy packs, touching hands to every square inch of burnt earth.

To endure mop-up, we played games. We asked would-you-rather questions, forcing a theoretical choice between horrible situations: would you rather walk around Manhattan holding hands with Bernie Madoff or play monopoly with Mike Tyson? Sometimes choices were topical to firefighting: would you rather walk five miles of Alaska tussock swamp or California bulldozer line? Mostly though, the questions were crass: would you rather get an erection in public or shit your pants?

In another game, one guy describes a perfect scene—girl-friend in pajamas, brunch, sunshine through the window, curled up on a comfy Saturday morning couch—and then everyone else subtly tears apart his idyllic world. It was theoretical gaslighting so diabolical you couldn't help but be impressed, and it wasn't for everyone. Some guys never seemed to grasp the fine balance of transforming something joyful into something miserable—for them, the game always ended with someone shitting their pants.

The games built camaraderie, but they also perpetuated machismo and tribalism. As the season dragged on, it grew harder and harder to locate the line between professionalism and the clique of the crew. People who fell out of favor were ostracized, sometimes for errors in communication, but more often for failing to demonstrate the specific mental and physical fitness that made it possible to endure months of tedious and backbreaking work.

A squad boss my rookie year liked to say that to succeed on fire, you needed to "channel the hate in your heart." The more time passes, the truer his words feel.

The day I received my job offer to work on a hotshot crew, I was building hiking trails with a conservation corps. I will never forget how the Forest Service liaison working with us responded to my news.

"I'm going to be a hotshot," I told my coworkers. "They said it's an elitist position."

The liaison must have had experience in fire because his sarcasm cut deep.

"You know elitist and elite don't mean the same thing, right?" he said.

In three seasons, I only worked with four women. Still, more than a few men complained that they couldn't be themselves with women around, or that women simply couldn't do the work. In my observation, the men most opposed to female crew members tended to be those whose own performances were criticized. They had been reprimanded for walking too slowly, for shoddy work, or for bad radio etiquette. Such men muttered under their breath like boys picked last at recess.

During my season out of Arizona, one of our vehicles broke down in Albuquerque, and we were given the night off to hit the town. After several rounds at the bar, a temporary crew member—they were all called "Phil" because they were fill-ins

and the bosses told us not to bother remembering their names—
flirted with a full-timer named Lindsey, one of the two women
on our crew. She rebuffed him, and he called her a bitch.

I watched as Lindsey slugged him and kept watching as our
boss, ferociously protective, punched the guy in the face. Someone
shoved the filler out the front door of the bar and slammed
him to the sidewalk. Lindsey had played soccer in college, and
she kicked him in the gut with her boot while two other crew
members pulled our boss away. A voice, I couldn't tell who it was
in the chaos, shouted, "Curb stomp the motherfucker!"

When we returned to base, the crew didn't see the filler again.
We didn't speak of the incident for the rest of the season, and
when I reached out to Lindsey years later for her memories of the
event, she said only that she thought it happened in California
and not Albuquerque. I'll never forget the violence of that scene,
and I may never make sense of the underlying drives behind it—
the drunk fill-in who used a horrible slur as response to a mild
rejection, the coworker who kicked him when he was down, the
boss who stormed off down the street and didn't speak to the
crew for two days afterward.

⟵——⟶

A few years passed between my season working in Arizona and
joining the crew in Alaska. I found crew culture in the North
even more exclusive and male. It took a while before I understood
the extra emphasis on toughness and strength as the product of a
belief in northern uniqueness.

Alaska fire is unique. For one, working in the boreal forest
means that you are fighting fire in a swamp. Mosquitoes can be
hellish. You work in ninety-degree heat, but your boots are always
wet. You cook your own food or eat military rations, MREs.

Crews from the Lower 48 sent on assignment to Alaska are even required to watch an orientation video, which includes advice on how to dig a latrine, build a tundra fridge, and shoot a problem bear. My boss in Arizona had described Alaska firefighting as horrible, "forty-three days of eating nothing but MREs."

But really, the job in Alaska isn't so different from fighting fire elsewhere. Your feet hurt, you carry heavy stuff, you walk in a straight line, and you eat bad food. For me, the work itself seemed pretty much the same as anywhere else until our assignment to Flat.

Flat embodies the white male narrative of Alaska as an eternal frontier almost perfectly. The ghost town was once the largest community in the state, with eight thousand inhabitants calling it home in the 1920s. Like so many of the gold towns in the Far North, though, as the minerals disappeared, so did the people, and it had long been abandoned.

In Flat, statewide fire management must have seen an opportunity to protect something with "real" historical value. To save Flat was to save the myth of the settler, to preserve the lie of rugged self-sufficiency and male strength. Our crew of white boys transformed into mythical frontier heroes, heading off to save Alaska's history from the onslaught of the wilderness. One afternoon the state head of forestry flew in for a tour. The fire was ten miles distant and moving away from the town, but it seemed we were doing the most important forestry work in the state.

In the two weeks before we flew to the ghost town, our crew had worked a fire that threatened an actual inhabited village. Lime Village was an old Dena'ina settlement way up the Stony River, with about twenty people still making their lives on the land. A fire had started in the expanse of boreal forest across the river from town.

It had been a tough roll. We'd herded the flame front toward a set of hills that sprouted out of the mosquito bogs, then deserted that plan when the fire jumped the Stony River on a windy day and churned off toward the Alaska Range, some hundred miles in the distance. We set up hoses and sprinklers throughout the town, and by the time we left the fire had grown from 10,000 to almost 250,000 acres.

The job changed with dizzying frequency. We worked direct fire line, dropping trees and running hoses along the fire's edge until the wind picked up. We coordinated burn operations in last-ditch efforts to cut off the main fire from its fuel source. When the heat passed, we crawled through burned ash and scoured the unburned edges, looking for hot spots that could rekindle with the next big gust of wind. We slept face down in the tussocks, our tents pitched on uneven swamp, too tired to give a damn.

It felt like worthwhile work, and we were glad to be getting paid overtime. The Lime Village school had closed the previous year. The loss of the school often marks the death knell for rural villages in Alaska, and the forest fire seemed like icing on the cake. We plumbed the town with hoses and water pumps, and I hoped we'd given them something more than just a means to keep things from burning down.

When we were reassigned, our departure felt to me like a betrayal of the community. The fire in Flat threatened some gold-mining relics and was burning miles away from the town, while the main flame front in Lime Village was sending spot fires only a half mile away from homes where people still lived. I wondered: is it more important to save the dead town or the dying one?

Maybe it depends on who is in charge.

←——————→

Our assignment in Flat was to assess structures and determine which parts of town were defensible against the wildfire. Since the entire valley had been dredge mined, the only trees growing were alders, which don't really burn well. The whole town had been churned to jagged gravel tailings; in another era, the whole valley would probably be labeled an EPA Superfund Site. Without much obvious work to do, we rummaged through homes looking for relics.

At one homestead, I made a list of what we found. It included several pairs of Sears overalls, a dismantled snowmachine up on blocks, a crumpled canvas tarp, Hills Bros. coffee cans filled with old machine parts, a Monarch brand vise, an anvil, White King laundry detergent, a *Time* magazine dated January 1966, a set of organized wrenches, cigar boxes, a butter keg, and a sheet metal frying pan. We found some old fishing equipment and spent a couple hours down at the creek catching grayling. One guy would fish while the others would keep lookout so we didn't get caught shirking.

The town hall was unlocked, and red, white, and blue bunting hung from a podium inside. We found two pianos, and though none of us could play, we plinked on the keys. When we left the building, our boot tracks lingered in the dust.

In a ghost town, where else would we find work besides the cemetery? We were tasked with cutting down every spruce tree in the graveyard. Even the unsuperstitious among us felt uneasy with the assignment.

Looking back now, I don't think we were there to do much about the fire. Cutting out alders around town and opening up graves to the sun helped preserve a sense of what Flat had been like in the days of brothels and miners. It allowed us to see the failed old mining town as still important.

On our third day, a family from California flew in. The wife had been raised in Flat, and she expressed gratitude for the work we were doing.

"I grew up playing on the dredges here," said the woman from California. Her husband thanked us for our service, and for cutting down all the trees in the cemetery.

After we cleaned up the cemetery, we started cleaning alders around an abandoned mining dredge. Before we began work, a group of us climbed up through the rusted hull and poked around the rusted machinery inside.

The sheer bulk of the machine intimidated me—the immensity of the engine, the ridiculousness of its purpose, the impossibility that it could be in this remote place, dragged across tundra for a hundred miles in an era before snowmachines and tractors. Here were pistons the height of upended cars, whole trees growing through the cylinders, buckets that could move seven hundred cubic tons of earth a day. The gray-lit air clung to the machine like an industrial fairytale. Gears and metal, gasoline and grease designed to extract glittering gold, left to rust.

I found a pair of coveralls hanging in the engine room, and I when I dug in the pockets, I found a tin of chewing tobacco. It still had a full pinch inside.

I shouted for the rest of the guys to come up. I shook the can and listened to fifty years of dust rattling in with the dried-out tobacco. I heard the others clanking around, and I imagined what would happen when they found the engine room.

I would tell everyone, "I found a forty-year-old tin of chew in these overalls."

"Twenty bucks if someone chews it," someone might say.

"You're being cheap," his saw partner would tell him.

A third would chime in. "If he does it, he has to gut the spit. You've gotta swallow it."

Then it would become a bet, debated, discussed, and logged with the bookkeeper.

Every fire crew I know of has a bookkeeper. We all keep notebooks stored in our pockets—sooty pages of information about fire behavior, weather patterns, first-aid protocols—but the bookkeeper keeps lists of every challenge and dare of the entire season. He writes down the rules for each bet, and he keeps a ledger of who has wagered. He is on hand whenever the occasion to try a bet might come along, and once a bet has been completed, he makes sure everyone pays their debts. On our crew, the bookkeeper was Ben.

A bet might start out something like this: It's late at night after a sixteen-hour shift. The crew should be in bed, but a hot spot popped up, so we get back into our boots instead of our sleeping bags, and after some quick scouting, we go direct—hot ash a mile long, creeping to the wind. Sometimes the fire gets into a thick stand of trees and jumps to the canopy, sends flames two hundred feet skyward. We retreat, wait for it to die down, and get back in. We cut burning trees into the black. We patrol the hillside all night, gridding for hot spots, pushing past twenty-four hours on our feet.

We anchor at the bottom of the hill and start hiking up. We're working double-time, and the fire keeps snaking around us and jumping our line, again and again, and soon someone is taking the blame for not doing the job right, and it's probably a rookie.

This poor guy hasn't showered in twelve days, he can't sleep, and he's constipated. He doesn't understand why there haven't been puppies to rescue, why his coworkers are so cynical, or why his boots never dry out. He's walked up and down the same hill a dozen times, probably carrying a cubee. He gags at the smell of his own clothes, and finally the rookie yells something he shouldn't.

"Fuck it, man!" he says, "I can't do this anymore! If I have to walk back up this hill one more fucking time, I will shit on my own face."

A veteran, the kind of guy who comes back year after year because, for him, fighting fire is better than summer camp, says, "I've got twenty on it."

At first, the rookie is confused. It's late, after all. He's tired.

"What?" he says.

"I'm taking the bet—if you walk up the hill again, you have to shit on your own face."

Someone else overhears. "I'd pay to see that—put me down for twenty too."

At first the bet seems like a big joke. Eventually, the crew catches the hot spot and gets some sleep. They spend the next day gridding up the hill, down the hill. Up and back down, in a line, over and over and over.

By lunch, the betting pot has grown to over two hundred bucks. By dinner, everyone has forgotten what precipitated the bet in the first place. The challenge has simplified. Nearly the entire crew has money riding on a single question: Will a man actually attempt to shit on his own face?

Several lines of inquiry emerge at this point. You ask yourself: How much money would it take to convince a guy to do such a thing? Who would pay money to watch that? Would I pay money to watch that? Is it even physically possible? How much money would it take for me to try?

At first, the rookie laughs it off. Absurd, he tells himself. He shakes his head at lunch, looks down and keeps quiet. But then one day, maybe a month or six weeks later, a few more assignments of wet feet, hard work, and big paychecks, somebody asks the bookkeeper to give a current state of the bet.

The bookkeeper has made note of all the debates, gambles, emotional shifts, and coping mechanisms. He has traced our descent and quantified it.

A June bet, a good one anyway—a shit-on-your-own-face kind of bet—will grow over the season. Someone who would never have considered gambling finds their bank account groaning with unspent cash, and on a slow day in late July, he might say, "Put fifty on that shit-on-the-face thing." By early August, the pot has climbed to almost two thousand dollars. The rookie starts to consider his options.

Twenty men on a hand crew. You can redefine the idea of heroism all you want, you can consider the damage such male posturing does to the psyche, but in the end, this bet is not hyperbole. It isn't a political statement or a metaphor for a crisis in masculinity. It's about what it takes to suck it up and eat shit. I had a hundred dollars on the rookie.

Inside the dredge's engine room, I imagined the inevitable— one guy vomiting, the laughter, the money exchanged at the end of the roll. In the dusky subarctic din, I thought about the world outside of the summer season, where success wasn't defined by the number of pull-ups I could do, and where heroism was far less complicated. I tucked the tin of Copenhagen back in the coveralls. In a month or two, I'd be nostalgic for this moment and this crew, but on that day, with the dry dust and tobacco cutting into my gums, I kept a few minutes for myself.

$$\longleftarrow \longrightarrow$$

The night before we flew out to Flat, our boss called everyone into a circle for an announcement. In Arizona, the Granite Mountain

Hotshot crew had been burned over in a fire outside Prescott. Everyone was dead.

Suddenly, the danger of the job, mostly forgotten amid the dull grind, kicked its way out of the world of hypotheticals. Tears welled up, and I fled from the group in search of my cell phone. Wade Tait had worked the previous season on Granite Mountain, and I didn't know if he was with the crew that year or not.

I worked on several fires with Granite Mountain when I was in Arizona. I remember we once shared a safety zone on the slopes of Mount Graham after the wind came up and we lost control of the fire. Our crews stood in a holding pattern for nearly three hours, sucking smoke, not allowed even to take a knee, monitoring the burned black so we didn't appear weak to one another.

Wade answered his phone when I called. He'd taken a job in Oregon that season. I knew this but had forgotten. Wade talked for a while about the men who died—good guys, he said. A good crew.

"It makes me worried. They're just like our crew," my crew boss said the next day when I landed with him in Flat. He meant: I'm responsible for you, and that kind of death could happen to us. He meant: I'm scared shitless.

A few months later, *Outside* magazine published an article on the Yarnell Fire tragedy. The article made an earnest effort to understand the last moments of the nineteen men who died, when they must have realized that their escape route and safety zones were gone, when the order to deploy came, and when they died of asphyxiation as temperatures around them roared above a thousand degrees.

What scared me most about the article was the similarities I saw with my own experiences on fire. How many times had I come to work a little hungover? How often had I grumbled and followed a crew boss, just assuming lookouts, communications, escape routes, and safety zones—the cornerstones of firefighting safety—were in place? How often had I felt the need to prove my physical ability when it made more sense to stand back? How often had I been told that the quality of our work reflected our self-worth? Granite Mountain, I thought, had consisted of men just like me.

←——————→

If I'm brutally honest with myself, it was easy to ignore the misogyny and prejudice. I loved the dirty jokes and tough guy posture. But when the curtain lifted, I was left questioning whether this hyperbolic masculinity could do what I needed it to do most—keep me alive.

In the Flat cemetery, I found the grave of the last person buried in the town. In place of a gravestone, a broad swath of a spruce tree trunk had been cut flat with a chainsaw. On the open slab, someone had burned the entire sixty-four lines of Robert Service's "Spell of the Yukon" into the wood.

The poem reminded me that I hadn't come to Alaska to live out a version of the Wild West dream. I came north because the landscape left me humbled. It makes me feel humble still. Today, what I miss most about fire are the landscapes—the long span of the Susitna River valley from the edge of tree line in the Alaska Range, helicopter blades dancing shadows above the Wrangell Mountains, a ridge in southern Utah that gave a glimpse of the canyonlands torn into the valley below.

Most of the people I worked with have also moved on from fire, into careers that won't leave them needing back surgery at age forty. Wade put in a few more seasons before he found a solitary job in an eastern Oregon lookout tower. Ben is now a fisheries biologist, and he performs as a balloon artist in his spare time. It has been a long time since any of us carried a cubee.

Part of me wants desperately to believe that the machismo inherent to the work I did during those years kept me safe, and that the work I did was heroic. Yet the more I look back, the less I trust the person I was back then. I wonder if fire simply gave my chauvinism a playground. I wonder if, like Ben's would-be Santa Claus, I, too, was corrupted by the work.

The journey from those idealistic days when I carried a measuring tape in my pocket to the final events that drove me away from the job doesn't follow a clear path. I still don't have an answer for the question Ben posed about his odd allegory. Perhaps every dysfunctional workplace has its own version of rookies fighting to carry the cubee. Or maybe there is no equivalent to the peculiar tribalism of fire. Nowhere else I have worked was competence determined by such primitive means.

Last of all, I remember the bears.

It is my rookie season, on a burn operation in the mountains of New Mexico. Our crew is using a two-track road near a Girl Scout camp to set a fire that would ignite a thousand acres of ponderosa forest and, hopefully, pull the main flame front away from the camp.

The burn boss checks wind, humidity. We mark our paces through smoke-drenched twilight. Drip torches flare. We scout for spot fires. I check my spacing as the line progresses, trailing fire that draws up the hillside to the smoking summit. My back broils against three-hundred-foot flames. Eyes unwrapped, I count verbs that describe smoke: billows, churns, roars. The operation crescendos to a tempest, and smoke stings, engulfs, suffocates, reveals my inadequacy.

It feels like vomiting Copenhagen after a lost bet, sucking down a hundred cigarettes a minute, snot drizzling into soot, salt smearing into my mouth, and I stand straight because posture is part of belonging.

The scream chills me. A black bear gallops from the flamefront, two mewling cubs trailing, paws burnt, hair scorched to the same charred slag as the trees. She pauses in the gravel, and in the glow of our burn, I see the wildness in her eyes. Two seconds, maybe three, and the sow and cubs disappear downhill. Sparks simmer in their pawprints.

We would save the Girl Scout camp, and the next day we would contain the fire. In a week we would be on to the next assignment, and in October we would finish out the season, bank accounts flush with cash.

The bears would die that night, I was sure.

Learn the Flowers

In the next century
or the one beyond that,
they say,
are valleys, pastures,
we can meet there in peace
if we make it.

To climb these coming crests
one word to you, to
you and your children:

stay together
learn the flowers
go light

—GARY SNYDER, "FOR THE CHILDREN"

*I*N THE DAPPLED sunshine, the current danced through a
spectrum of colors. Thick glacial silt churned like a lava lamp,
roiling from azure to slate to a green that glistened like gold.

We stood on a gravel bar of the Muskwa River, just downstream
from the Alaska Highway bridge. The previous night, my friend
Wade Tait and I had made camp near a waterfall, where we
watched a mountain goat prance over the canyon ledge near

our tent. That morning we'd driven into Fort Nelson, parked my dilapidated car at the airport, and loaded our gear—fishing rods, sleeping bags, tent, food, hatchet, Dutch oven, paddles, lifejackets, shotgun—into the canoe I had bought off a classified ad in Minneapolis. Over the course of the next two months we would drift, naïve and jewel-eyed, through a world of endless daylight down the Mackenzie River system to the edge of the Arctic Ocean.

Wade and I had concocted our journey the previous summer working together on a wildland fire crew. It was August, we'd been months in the heat and dust, and on a long drive to yet another fire, unshaven, still covered in ash from the last assignment, we pulled out an atlas, traced a thick blue line to the edge of the page, and decided a paddling trip seemed like a better adventure for the next year than walking through burning forests. Wade said he would meet me if I could sort out the logistics. I spent much of the winter planning food, searching for a boat, and buying gear; I even raised a little money for charity as part of the journey. Still, when Wade showed up mid-June as promised, I still didn't have a clear picture of what we planned to do. We just climbed into the car and drove north.

Three days in, a fishing rod tangled in a strainer and splintered. Two weeks of rain brought the mosquitoes up from the muskeg and had us cooking in the canoe to escape their horror. Our saturated maps became unreadable, our sleeping bags molded, the shotgun barrel rusted. I sunk a fishhook past the barb into my middle finger. One night we forgot the case containing our passports and car keys on the canoe thwart. The river rose as we slept and carried it away.

I dropped my camera in the great glut of the Liard River at flood stage and jumped in after it. Only later did I notice the trees bobbing beside our boat, torn from the riverbank by the sucking current. A woman in Fort Simpson gave us a gift of moose meat, but we left the bag in our canoe, and village dogs stole it. In Norman Wells, we left our boat unattended at the boat landing and returned to find half our food gone, eaten by a bear who dozed in the willows a few yards from the boat. Near Tulita, a storm came up, and after a full day sitting on a sandbar, we decided to brave the river. Seven-foot rollers flushed silty sludge across our boat. We bailed and paddled and prayed and only reached the opposite bank through sheer luck.

When I read my journals from the river trip today, I'm embarrassed by my naivety. I see a stranger full of machismo, who, having braved a little bad weather and some mosquitoes, claimed to know as much about the river as a local. In the mishaps of that trip, I see example after example of my own fragility. Mostly, I think I'm lucky my stupidity didn't get me killed.

I viewed paddling the river as a grand adventure and was convinced that the mishaps were part of the fun. I brought a copy of Alexander Mackenzie's journals, and read of his efforts to hunt swans, connect with the Indigenous residents, and figure out where in the hell he was. Of the locals, he wrote,

> it will be sufficient just to mention their attempts to per-
> suade us that it would require several winters to get to the
> sea, and that old age would come upon us before the period
> of our return: we were also to encounter monsters of such
> horrid shapes and destructive powers as could only exist in
> their wild imaginations.

So deep was my ignorance that I persuaded myself there was more to learn in the racist scribbles of a dead imperialist than in listening and learning from the actual experiences of people we met. Like Mackenzie, I didn't realize I was the butt of more than a few village jokes. Wade wouldn't touch the book.

Back then I held nomadism as the highest ideal toward which a person could strive, each journey a quest fraught with trials to conquer. I believed that despite my posturing on a fire crew, my deluded pilgrimages, and the errant certainty that I could go wherever I wanted because somehow, through faith or family or because I'd read a lot of books, I was different. It took me a long time to realize I was simply running away.

Only now, in marriage and fatherhood, have I realized how floating the Mackenzie River nurtured an essential element of my inner self—by balancing my daily life with the rhythm of the seasons, I was becoming attuned to place.

One day, three men motored up to the gravel bar where Wade and I were eating lunch. They asked if we had seen any moose. We hadn't. They saw our shotgun, which we kept for bears, and asked if we had seen any ducks. A flock happened to be floating past. The two younger men jumped back into their boat.

"Come on," they said, and I grabbed the shotgun and followed. They positioned me on the bow, revved the motor, and shouted "Shoot!" as the birds rose from the water. I fired round after round, and we chased the flock up and down the river, motor roaring, until we had three birds in the boat.

"It's easier this way," said one of the men, explaining the not-exactly-ethical, or legal, technique.

Back on shore, the old hunter shook his head and smiled. "Now we don't have enough gas to go back upstream to our village," he said and added that they hadn't brought much food or gear since they'd only planned to be out for a day.

The thought that they suddenly had no way home floored me. It was another 150 miles to the next downstream settlement; Wade and I wouldn't make it there for almost a week. Yet the old man seemed nonchalant. Wade asked if he was worried about having to walk home. He shrugged and pointed to a forest that stretched unbroken to the Atlantic Ocean. He was already home.

When we embrace the endless light and momentary danger of rivers that can be paddled only three months a year, northern landscapes can reflect our most private thoughts. Every eddy, rock, oxbow, strainer, rapid, and silted sandbar, impediments to the river's seaward traverse, became part of a conversation with water. The campfires that baked bread or fried fish, the campsites where we slept, and the tangled thickets of black spruce where we walked in the evenings formed a dialogue with the land. Long weeks with the motion of a paddle were teaching me how to listen.

We floated past a cabin about seventy-five miles downriver from the confluence of the Liard and the main stem of the Mackenzie. A man was pulling in his fishing net with a skiff, and he killed the motor to ask where we were from. He disentangled a pike from his net and tossed it in our boat.

"Here, for dinner," he said. The fish he gave us was the only one he had caught. We shouted our thanks as the current spun us downriver.

After a month, Wade and I ran out of conversation. I would point out a flock of ducks. He would nod. I would ask him what kind of beer he was going to order when we reached Inuvik.

Wade would grunt. One day I begged him to talk, asked him how I'd offended him. An hour later, he finally replied, "Being silent doesn't mean I'm angry."

Two more days went by before he spoke again.

We had reached a state of torpor, and in that quiet, we saw a yearling black bear attack a pair of nesting sandhill cranes. We watched a falcon attack a goose and freefall with its prey into the current. We glimpsed moose, eagles, a lynx and her cub. Once, we spied a wolverine feeding on a moose carcass. When we drifted close, it dragged the remains up the ten-foot cutbank.

Riding on the unharnessed power of a great river, I couldn't quite fathom the immensity of the landscape. The Mackenzie is so big that it creates its own weather, pushes the boreal forest beyond the northern tree line to the edge of the Arctic Ocean. The hydrology and geology of the watershed, from the glacial beginnings in the mountains to the sprawling delta, demand a connection that goes well beyond floating the current for a summer. Loving the river requires an act of faith.

We reached Inuvik in mid-August and spent a week at the town campground, savoring this outpost town as a return to civilization. One evening, a local man named John Tsul wandered into our campsite. He was trying to sober up and seemed to have decided that telling stories to two white guys would help. He took us into the forests around town and showed us how to gather spruce gum and Labrador tea. He talked about his trapline, about ancient wars between Gwitch'in and Inuvialuit people that stretched back centuries, about a nearby lake where hundreds of people had died in a great battle, their bodies sunk to the bottom. He said the lake was so haunted nobody dared swim in it. He told horror stories about his time as a NATO soldier during the Bosnian War, punctuating his speech with long silences and pursed whistles. He even had a joke about a hunter who gave a hand job to a polar bear.

John Tsul was Métis, and he embodied my vision of what it meant to live in the Far North. I held his stories on a pedestal for years after and retold them to people as lessons, as if I had discovered a purer truth, a right way to learn how to live here.

I remember the last story he told, about a mean village dog who had licked his hand. The owner couldn't believe that the dog hadn't bit him.

"You gotta be good to him," John Tsul had said to the man. He stopped his story and looked hard at Wade and me.

"That's the key, right there," he said. "Be kind, and it'll all come back to you."

We left town the next day, having sold our canoe to a guy in town on a Watson grant to study river deltas. We caught a ride to the Dempster Highway with a man on his way to the airport, he said, to pick up a truckload of frozen seals. We stuck out our thumbs, jumped in a van with an Australian couple, and sped south. We left the river valley and rolled across open tundra for hundreds of miles, back below the Arctic Circle into Dawson. It took another week of hitchhiking to reach our car, which had a dead battery—though we'd at least stuck a spare key in the wheel well. We drove hard for three days to reach Vancouver and spent an afternoon convincing customs officials to let us cross the border without passports. Wade and I parted ways outside Seattle. I turned east and he rolled south.

In the far margins where we had traveled, where cartographers once wrote "here be dragons" on their maps, where John Tsul's stories resided, I felt a sense of belonging I couldn't shake. I spent the next several months in the Southern Hemisphere, and even at the bottom of the world, I found myself looking at maps, following road lines out beyond the interstate highways that ran like veins across the center of North America. I longed for the capillary paths, the roads that trickled north, into the boreal forest and beyond.

The following year, during the early days of the spring thaw, I found a seasonal job in Alaska. I enrolled in graduate school in Fairbanks for the fall semester. In late summer, I loaded as much stuff as I could fit in a car and moved north permanently. In the years since arriving here, I find fewer and fewer reasons to leave.

Since becoming a father, I've begun to put more stock in the idea of fate. When I try to render the memories of my years spent abroad, bicycling through hot countries full of palm trees, wandering among the ruins of ancient cultures, and eating cheap street food in some sort of search for authenticity, it seems silly that I tried to form connections with places I had no business being, and where I never stayed longer than a day or two.

I have memories, sure; mostly they are of people. There was the week spent chasing an alleged orangutan kickboxing ring on the Cambodian border with a British man who rescued elephants for a living. I remember a mustachioed nun along the Lebanese coast who made us coffee with quaking hands and sang the Easter troparion in Slavonic. I still have the postcards from a guy in the mountains of British Columbia who claimed to be searching for a "rainbow bear"—a mythical black bear whose fur color was a hybrid between the ghost-colored Kermode bear and the blue-hued glacier bear, variants themselves so rare in those snowy peaks as to be nearly mythological as well. My mouth waters for the pizza I had on the far side of Isla de Ometepe, made by a Nicaraguan chef who had worked at the top restaurants in New

York City but abandoned city life for a shack in the jungle and an earthen oven.

In my journals, I imagined I was encountering seers and mystics on those journeys. Mostly, though, I met storekeepers, other tourists, quacks. On the Mackenzie River, and even when I first settled in Alaska, I relished my status as an outsider. I still believed that to find my path, I had to escape familiar society like a fourth-century monastic.

Only now, years later, do I see the roadways of my journeys for what they were: lessons in learning to accept my weaknesses. I discovered quickly that Arctic rivers are the lifeblood of this continent, but it has taken me far longer to learn that the people of the North are its soul. It is the people we build relationships with, and the communities we depend on to sustain us, that teach us the true rhythms of our lives.

The spring job that brought me to Alaska was based in Talkeetna. I spent the spring collecting sap from birch trees to make into syrup. Working so closely with the wild bounty of the Far North, I might have seen the value of living a life defined by place. Instead, I crashed a snowmachine, got lost along a river, and broke up with my girlfriend, who had also come up to work. That summer I flew to Istanbul and bicycled for two months. I got back together with my ex before returning to Fairbanks for graduate school. We drove up together, broke up again. And still I kept dreaming of the next adventure.

I gathered a few berries that fall and moved into a dry cabin for the winter. The next summer, I caught and canned a dozen salmon. In August I went hunting and harvested a caribou. When my second winter came, the shelves in my cabin groaned under the weight of home-canned food. Slowly, I was learning to be critical of the nomad narrative I had created for myself. In embracing the uniqueness of life lived according to a seasonal cycle of abundance and scarcity, I discovered that even nomads— maybe especially nomads—survived by building an intimacy with the ecology of place.

Living in Fairbanks brought about another connection: I met Mollie. She lived in a dry cabin down the road, and I had a serious crush on her. Unfortunately, my affection was unrequited. Mostly, I think Mollie was just grateful I helped her whenever her dog—a gorgeous husky who made winter skijoring a dream and regularly ran off to chase moose and wander the neighborhood—escaped. We hiked, skied, drank beers at the campus pub together, and spent nearly three years dating other people before we fell in love with each other.

Despite the platonic nature of it, my friendship with Mollie made me feel connected in ways I couldn't quite explain— though looking back, it does help me understand why every romantic relationship I had during those years ended in failure. A connection must have grown inside Mollie too. When we finally started dating, it felt right away like finding a soulmate.

For our honeymoon, we paddled seven hundred miles of the Yukon River. We had just navigated a week of intense wedding preparation, confusing Russian Orthodox rituals, and rowdy relatives. It felt good to move at a quieter pace, where the physical journey down the river served as muse for conversations about the journey of building a life together.

By then I had learned some things about these big northern rivers and landscapes. Mollie and I had paddled together—in the Everglades and in Alaska—long enough that steering the canoe came as naturally as breathing, our paddle strokes part of a collective muscle memory. We never camped near bear sign. We always entered an eddy facing upstream when we pulled to shore. When the wind came up or a thunderstorm threatened, we pitched the tent well up from the water and waited it out. Most days, the river's motion served as meditation. We bladed for hours as we scanned the hillsides for feeding bears.

We brought our dog Magnolia along—the same dog who during our time in graduate school had been so fond of escaping to explore the town. She dozed on top of our packs as we approached Five Finger Rapids, where rollers channeled the river through a series of rocky outcrops. Mollie navigated the run so smoothly that the dog never even woke up. We ate pike and grayling, searched feeder creeks for salmon smolts. We passed the ruins of old towns, trapper and miner cabins, abandoned paddle-wheelers. We counted bears, swans, moose, and even mule deer. Near Calico Bluff, we watched a wolf sunning on a gravel bar.

In the end, our trip down the Yukon didn't feel like an adventure, but a contemplative retreat. I was finally learning, like the monk who carried the stone in his mouth, that the most important part of my body is my ears.

Our first summer as a couple, Mollie was living in a cabin outside Homer handling sled dogs, and I was fighting forest fires, living in a wall tent along the Knik River five and a half hours away. When a distant relative pitched a job teaching high school in a rural district on the Missouri-Arkansas border, we met up in the Palmer City Park and debated whether to leave Alaska. The offer only guaranteed work for me, but the relative promised he could get a job for Mollie, too, teaching foreign language. It seems obvious now that we never should have taken work so clearly a bad fit for both of us, especially since Mollie had a lot of reservations about the idea, but at the time, it felt like a chance at stability. I pushed the decision, and she eventually agreed.

Actually, bad fit is an understatement. The school had a student body with some of the lowest literacy rates in the nation, and general attitudes among teachers and staff toward the kids ranged from indifferent to openly hostile. The bizarre pride, indifference, and simmering violence that served as defining features of the abject rural poverty in the area scared me. The job promised to Mollie never appeared, and she ended up an elementary school reading tutor. We spent our nights arguing, trying to justify reasons to stay, equal parts guilt ridden and resentful, unable to figure out where we'd go if we left.

Still, when we were run out of the county by the school superintendent for complaining about a school training in which off-duty police officers shot blank ammunition at teachers, it felt like a searing betrayal. Thrown to the wolves by the family member who had convinced us to move there and shaken by the politics of education in rural America, we turned to the woods.

For six months, we walked the length of the Appalachian Trail, from Georgia to Maine. By September, our bodies felt like wire cables bent too many times: strong but frayed and ready to snap. Our bank accounts empty, we beat back winter on a long autumn drive back north to the hills above Homer, Alaska. We didn't quite know it then, but we were headed home.

We took work as dog handlers and moved into a sixteen-by-sixteen-foot dry cabin with thirty huskies just outside our front door. When Mollie and I merged our lives, dogs were part of the deal. Our three pups could be a lot to manage at times, but I quickly learned that life in a dog yard is a different thing entirely. Beyond the feeding, the madness of harnessing for a run, and the endless amounts of poop to scoop, we had to keep apprised of the ever-changing social minutiae of the dog world: which dogs were in heat and which dogs were bored, sick, or getting on each other's nerves. When katabatic winds tore down the glaciers across Kachemak Bay and ice storms rose up the hillside into the dog yard, we pulled on our gear and went out to make sure everyone was warm and dry.

Good snow never really came that year, so we spent most of the winter helping hook teams to a four-wheeler. When a job opened at a community college two hours north of Homer, I applied, and to my surprise they hired me. One day in the spring, we took our three dogs for a hike along the beach, and I asked Mollie to marry me. She said yes.

A couple of months later, we found an ad on Craigslist for a cabin near where I would work. We drove up on a Saturday to look at the place and decided that day to buy it. There was a sauna out back, a garden with raspberries, flowerbeds, and a homesteader aesthetic. From the beginning, it felt like a place to be a family. By end of summer, we were property owners in way over our heads.

The house needed a lot of work. Every water fixture in the house leaked, including a double-wide jacuzzi tub and an on-demand heater that didn't heat. The septic system ran out to a collapsed hole in the ground behind the house. The breaker box was mounted in a crawlspace under the stairs and wired up with—I swear I'm serious—masking tape.

We set about fixing up the place. We paid people to put in a proper septic system, and we converted a crumbling tarp structure in the yard into a serviceable woodshed. We converted the basement into a brewing room. We learned there is a big difference between trying to emulate some Alaskan ideal in a

Fairbanks dry cabin and actually living like an adult in the North.

In Alaska I have found my childhood dreamscape, a place with a lifetime of knowledge to gain, adventures to undertake, horizons to explore. I hunt, fish, and forage. I can identify a good number of the plants and name key topographic features. I love living here, but it takes more than fixing the drainpipes to forge real connection, and often, I still feel like a drifter.

The more I discover about the Alaska—this place I want so badly to belong to—the more I realize my ideas about home and travel still have a lot of maturing to do. Sometimes I dream of the cities, mountains, and seascapes I moved through during those wandering years, but I no longer see those places as exotic. The strange looks people gave me as I walked through the markets in rural Asian villages came because I was the exotic presence in their lives and not the other way around. Despite my best efforts, as a white man in the North, I'm still a foreigner.

I have discovered that there is a correct way to love a landscape, but money, industry, tourism—all the usual damages and cruelties inflicted on colonized places—make finding a narrative that includes me seem impossible. I often worry that the ways I have learned to inhabit the North just perpetuates the colonialism. I wonder whether I'm much different than Mackenzie, if I'm seeing from the same skewed perspective he did when he passed through in 1789.

Consider: almost six years after I was in Inuvik, I ran in to John Tsul again. I recognized him hitchhiking on the side of the road outside Watson Lake, British Columbia. He was headed to Edmonton to see his sister. I gave him a ride, and I tried to explain the impression that his stories and insights had left on me when we'd first met. I told him that I'd tried to tell the polar bear joke once, and it had failed.

He told me the joke about the polar bear again. He said he had to get out of the North for a while. I asked him about trapping. He said that he'd had a bad season, hadn't even made it out to his line, had spent the winter in Inuvik and the summer in Fort McPherson trying to sober up. I dropped him off in Edmonton at a diesel truck repair shop on the edge of the city where his sister worked. We didn't shake hands. We didn't exchange numbers. I drove on.

←——————→

Just before I moved to Alaska, I stayed in Istanbul for a week with an American expat named Jim. One day, Jim took me and his mother on a tour of the city's mosques and churches. We took ferries across the Bosporus, hopped trains and buses, marveled at blue mosaics while Jim expounded on the architectural fluidity of Ottoman religious buildings. Later, we walked through the alleyways of the Golden Horn where we stopped to check out a small church near the home of the Patriarch of Constantinople, the spiritual leader of Orthodox Christianity across the globe. We arrived too late to visit the parish but just in time to see Patriarch Bartholomew, flanked by security guards, climbing into a black sedan.

The car stopped next to us, and the driver stepped out to open the rear door. The patriarch beckoned us to the car. I bowed my head, and he pressed a bracelet of prayer beads into my hand. He handed the same gift to Jim's mother. When Jim stepped in for a blessing, however, the Patriarch couldn't find another bracelet. Finally, he rummaged through his cassock, pulled out his keys, and removed a small LED light from the keychain. He demonstrated it by clicking the switch on and off several times, then handed it over.

"A light," said the Patriarch, "to shine." The car pulled away and he was gone.

I told that story to my coworker, friend, and mentor Alan Boraas not long before he died in 2019. Alan was one of Alaska's most respected anthropologists, and one of the most gifted, empathetic thinkers I have ever known—a man who fought for land and subsistence rights regardless of the consequences, who understood that the people who have lived in a place longest generally have the most to teach us about how best to reside there.

He thought about my story for a long time before he replied.

"You really only need a flashlight for about half the year up here," he said. We laughed, but then Alan added that if you know a place well enough, you didn't need a light at all. He told me about a ski trip he took once where he'd gotten caught out near dark in unfamiliar country but made his way home because the Dena'ina place names, which he had studied, for the lakes and ridgelines where he was traveling had directions embedded in them. Knowing the land had kept him safe.

I thought just then of John Tsul. We hadn't been friends, I realized. I remember once he'd referred to outsiders as "tourer-ists." To him I was an outsider. He had shared stories with me for his own reasons, not out of some benevolent desire to teach me about the North. Suddenly, I felt like a trespasser, working on the border again, a voyeur.

Alan's work on Indigenous spirituality makes the claim that "we elevate to the sacred those things that are most important in our lives." He believed that people needed to spend time with a place, nurturing it and navigating it, to have a real relationship with that place.

In a world where we have hacked away at our own roots, it isn't easy to develop personal connections. The cohesive narrative that we envision—the one about finding ourselves and our faith, about healing and purpose and our own little slice of paradise—distorts the reality and complexity of just being present. When we never stop searching, the balance of our lives never quite reaches equilibrium.

Too often I have sought reinvention by moving from place to place without pausing to reflect; I tear off one mask only to find another underneath. I have embarked on quest after quest to address problems created because I wasn't willing to simply be still. I am still learning to be homesick.

Perhaps it matters less what we do than it matters how we connect with the place where we choose to do it. Whether we seek answers in the dark corners of foreign cities or a dilapidated cabin, we must first learn how to look. Sure, it helps to carry a flashlight, but the real trick, I think Alan would say, is to simply know where you are.

Other Bloods

*I*N AUGUST, BEYOND northern tree line, above the Arctic Circle, past the edges of black spruce tottering and drunk on permafrost, where the sage smell of Labrador tea rises from the ground and the mountains fall away and tundra rolls to the Beaufort Sea, the central Arctic caribou herd departs from their coastal breeding grounds, heading south on their fall migration.

In 2011, on my first hunt in Alaska, I came up the Dalton Highway to follow this herd and try to fill my freezer. I drove up from Fairbanks with three other men. We planned to hunt along the road and pipeline corridor, parallel ribbons of gravel and oil a hundred miles north of Atigun Pass, where the animals sometimes travel.

This first trip was a strange introduction to the world of hunting in Alaska. I had just finished a season fighting wildland fire, a season full of testosterone, and I hoped that this trip would bring me a chance for a quieter kind of interaction with a landscape I was quickly falling in love with. Instead, I found myself crammed into a truck, driving up and down a 150-mile corridor of road, looking out the window for passing animals.

Two of my companions, Rick and Wayne, were FBI agents posted to Alaska. Wayne came from Chicago and was obsessed with big antlers; as far as I could tell, he spent most of his paychecks on hunting and hadn't yet managed to shoot anything. Rick came from South Carolina. He'd grown up hunting, and he reminded me of a taciturn and honorable lawman from TV. The third guy, Ryan Ragan, was a fellow graduate student who had relocated his family to Alaska so he could pursue mountain man ambitions of fishing, hunting, and writing poetry about Bigfoot. Ryan attended church with Rick out near the car dealerships on the south side of Fairbanks and had invited me on this hunt as a kindness.

All three men wore Gore-Tex camouflage clothing, ate freeze-dried meals, and had been on dozens of hunts. I wore a plaid wool shirt, and I ate jars of smoked salmon. I'd hunted grouse and deer a few times, but that was it.

We camped near a weather station north of Toolik Lake, and in the evening, they ate their meals from plastic bags and watched me eat cold salmon from the jar. Wayne talked for a long time about his weakness for Latina women. He'd been divorced at least twice. Rick said that we would get to punch our man cards for camping out on open tundra. I had an image of a Man Card certificate, framed, mounted, and punched full of holes, hanging in a cubicle. I felt left out of something important—something maybe I should have purchased at Bass Pro Shop before we left. I commented on the stark beauty of the Arctic.

"I can't get over the colors of the tundra," I said. "It reminds me of an expressionist painting." Ryan laughed. The FBI agents fell silent. Apparently, I wouldn't be getting a punch on my man card.

Regulations don't allow rifle hunting within five miles of the highway; off-road vehicle access is also illegal. Ryan and Wayne had compound bows, which meant they could stay close to the road and hunt within eyeshot of the pickup. With only my rifle,

I faced a long hike in and out, and I was the only one with much interest in walking.

My companions wanted to keep driving, looking for easy shots and caribou with bigger antlers. During the week we hunted, the main herd was nowhere near the road. The few caribou that did turn up spooked at the sound of the truck. We saw musk oxen. We checked out the oil fields in Prudhoe.

Twice we found caribou close enough to approach, but both times they managed to get away. On our first day, we came across a lone bull, and Ryan and Rick followed it along a creek bed, while Wayne and I took off across an exposed hill. I managed to get close but didn't have a bow. By the time Wayne caught up, the bull had spooked, and we watched it disappear into the expanse.

The next morning, we found a small herd and repeated the maneuver. This time Wayne and I followed the road up to the top of a rise. I crouched low in the willows and stayed quiet. Within a minute or two, the caribou herd passed just twenty yards from where I sat, crossed the road, and meandered off. When I looked around to see why nobody had taken a shot, I found Wayne rummaging around the back of the truck. He'd forgotten to put arrowheads on his arrows.

"All the animals were small anyway," he said later. "I'm looking for a trophy."

I was starting to feel claustrophobic in the backseat. I hadn't come six hundred miles to drive around. So after a couple of days driving, I asked if they would mind if I hiked out beyond the five-mile corridor to hunt alone for a night.

"If you get something, come back to the road, we'll find you," Ryan said.

I felt released, hopeful, a little scared I would actually succeed. I set out, thinking about Thoreau and Robert Frost and solitude, and about Raven stories. In my short time in Alaska, I had found the presence of ravens everywhere. In the dumpsters on the edge of town, in stories shared by old Native ladies at community potlucks at the Mushers Hall in Fairbanks, in the artwork that decorated the university library where I studied. I had learned that in northern cultures, hunting stories are often raven stories, and that sometimes the birds follow the caribou herds. The raven, they say, is a trickster, sometimes bringing luck and sometimes taking it.

I walked beneath the pipeline towering over my head. I looked for pingos—mounds of uplifted permafrost—and felt the mossy mattress under my boots. From the top of ridgelines, I watched the cut of crystalline rivers that stretched to far horizons, and I watched for circling ravens.

Hunting isn't for everyone, and not all hunters are alike. It is an individualistic activity by nature, and each hunter has a different way of justifying why they hunt. For some—especially out-of-state doctors and executives with too much money—hunting amounts to a measuring contest over who has the biggest antlers. These folks pay for bush flights that drop them a half day in front of the main herd. They hire a guide, camp for a night, wake up to freshly brewed coffee and a thousand animals streaming past. Their guide dresses the animal, and they pay to have a butcher shop cut the meat with pork and make summer sausage for their buddies back home. They have the heads mounted on a reception room wall as a demonstration of their conquest.

At the other end of the spectrum, for the Indigenous people whose relationship with moose and caribou stretches back to the Ice Age, hunting isn't just an activity; it is a way of life. But it is even more than that. For the myriad Indigenous people of the North who hunt for subsistence, the connection to hunting runs so deep that the idea of a diet without moose or caribou is inconceivable.

On my first visit to the Far North, I ran into a young white woman in Inuvik, Northwest Territories. She was from Ontario and a vehement vegetarian. When she learned that the people in the Mackenzie River delta hunted caribou, moose, musk oxen, and beluga whale as the main foods for their local diet, she was horrified.

I said, "We're above the Arctic Circle. What are people supposed to eat?"

"Vegetables," she replied. "Maybe once they had to eat helpless animals to survive, but they should change with the times."

Her comment rubbed me the wrong way, but at the time, I didn't know enough to explain why. Not until years later, living in Alaska amid political battles about the never-ending oil and mine proposals that threaten salmon streams and caribou herds did I come across an explanation that summed up how important subsistence hunting is to original residents of a place.

Jacquelyn Ross, an Indigenous scholar, writes about the importance of traditional food and health among Native communities. For Native people, she says, the loss of traditional food "is bigger than the problem of the children thinking that milk comes from cartons. . . . It is unjust for people not to be able to have their native foods."

For some cultures and communities, hunting isn't a pastime. Moose and caribou, and the lands that sustain those animals, are as necessary to survival as a heartbeat.

←——→

I want to believe that my own reasons for hunting fall somewhere in the middle, but the longer I inhabit this state, this landscape I can't quite call home, the less sure I am about wanting to shoot and eat the animals that live here. I love the earthy and herbal flavor of caribou meat, but I have at best a fleeting relationship with the animals. Alaska is a big place, and I drive hundreds of miles to reach legal hunting areas. Moose reside closer to home but are harder to hunt. When I'm in the woods with a gun and I stop to think about how many Alaskans—mostly Indigenous folks—still rely on wild meat for subsistence, I start to feel like I'm trespassing. When I think about the way adjectives like *recreational* and *sport* function as legal terms to describe killing, I start to feel a little unethical.

I must confess something else: even now, having hunted in the wild places of Alaska each fall for almost a decade, I am not a very good hunter. I grew up in northern Wisconsin, a place where manliness is still determined by the size of the antlers on your dead November buck. The first whitetail I ever managed to shoot was missing an antler. Talk about emasculation.

When I come across coveys of ptarmigan while bird hunting, even though they're pretty stupid birds you can often shoot on the ground, I rarely shoot them because I like to watch them fly, to watch them disappear in midair because their white wings so perfectly reflect the snow.

In tree stands, I spend most of my time reading a book. I don't like to wake up early. I'm easily distracted by the patterns of frost on a leaf in the morning. And worst of all, I can't sit still. After about an hour, I start to fidget, hum, sing, or otherwise notify every animal in a ten-mile radius of my presence. If the early bird gets the worm, then the hyperactive hunter buys meat from the grocery store.

Still, I love hunting, and I love caribou hunting most of all. For a guy like me, who craves the walking as much as I enjoy the harvest of meat, caribou offer a near perfect experience. They don't spook that easily and they are always moving. Some herds will travel more than three thousand miles between the tundra plains and the boreal forests where they shelter each winter. After I left my hunting companions in the truck, I hiked over a dozen miles—glassing with binoculars and thinking—before I saw an animal.

Walking, I saw the tracks of caribou traced on the barren ground, their antlers scattered across a thousand years of migration trails. I buried my hands into the moss and felt permafrost just below the surface. I kicked through tussock, tasted with cupped hands the Kuparuk River—icy shimmering glass, where dark outlines of grayling hovered in the shallow pools. When I glimpsed a lone bull in the distance, I wondered how it could stay so well-camouflaged in such openness.

I think part of my love for hunting stems from my love of stories. The trajectory of a hunt often feels like the plotline of a well-crafted mystery. The tension rises like Freytag's Pyramid, plot twists and character developments guiding us from the empty freezer to the open tundra. Red herrings, missed chances, muscle cramps, dehydration, and sparse dialogue spin the story toward an uncertain climax.

The experience of a hunt balances poetry and myth. The quiet patterns of feet and breathing that arc over the journey, from the lichen-covered rocks to the gut pile, contain a broken symmetry like a metered line. Stalking an animal and writing a good poem require the same instincts.

In the years since I have taken up hunting with seriousness, I've felt the powerful relationship between hunter, prey, and land more often on unsuccessful trips. Sure, I enjoyed the days when I headed out in the morning for the mountains north of Fairbanks, found caribou a quarter mile into the legal hunting area, and had meat hanging by lunchtime. But those hunts are rare. Only twice have I been so lucky, and both times it felt like cheating.

Once, I floated the Fortymile River with a bull moose harvest tag during five bluebird days in September. A handful of old dredge miners were cleaning up their summer camps for the season, but mostly, I had the river to myself. I had never shot a moose then, and I had no real inkling of what I'd do if I got one.

Fortunately, I only saw cow moose and caribou. Mostly, I climbed to vantage points and looked out on country so raw it took my breath away. I camped under yellowing birch trees, drifted along the black current, and marveled at how a place that seemed so close to the far edge of the world could make me feel so centered. I crawled up deep gorges that spilled tundra out of their rims. One afternoon, I was following a game trail up a creek drainage toward a black spruce pasture when the brush ahead of me crackled with noise.

I dropped to my knees and readied my rifle. I kept my breathing silent and even. After a while, an enormous bull caribou emerged through a break in the alders, less than ten yards from where I crouched. He was shedding the velvet growth of his antlers; it ribboned over his brow in bloody strands. His neck muscles twitched with signs of the coming rut. I set down my rifle and, centimeter by centimeter, rose to a standing position. Still the bull didn't move. For perhaps five minutes we faced one another, the air between us bristling with an unseen current. I tried to send him thoughts across the void of air. "Thank you," I wanted to tell him. Finally, he exhaled a deep breath and resumed clacking along his migration route. My eyes had welled over, pouring tears because I had forgotten to blink.

I read later in the late anthropologist Richard Nelson's book *Make Prayers to the Raven* that caribou are the only animals Koyukon Athabaskan hunters sing to. I wish I had known to sing to that bull.

On another hunt, I called in two bull moose to the meadow where I sat. The larger one crashed through thick brush toward my imitation moans, the smaller bull grunting at his heels. I was hunting in an area with antler size restrictions, and neither moose was quite legal. I stood up. They kept loping toward me, coming twenty, then ten, then five yards away, and I ducked behind the only cover around, a tiny spruce sapling. It wasn't protection; the moose towered over me. I had to start talking to get them to stop.

"I'm a human," I said. "I'm sorry."

They didn't leave. For the next half hour, the pair rutted around the field, snorted, circled, locked horns, fought. I could smell the heavy musk of their urine and see steam shedding the damp from their shoulders in the golden evening light. When they finally headed off and my adrenaline had stabilized, I felt like a drunk after closing time.

I am always aware that the likelihood of coming home with meat is slim. Sometimes I've returned home with berries instead of meat. Bad weather has stymied a few trips. I have watched Dall sheep play on snowfields, spooked bears as they ambled through the brush, spied swans practicing for their winter trip south. I have been cold, hot, wet, dehydrated. Whether I return home successful or not, I always feel that the land and the deliberate watching of the microcosms of a place rejuvenates me. Often, hunting seems like a gift of grace.

Anytime I step into the woods with even an inkling that I might kill something, I am toying with powers beyond rational understanding. I've come to believe that on some level only luck, living luck born of respect and proper behavior toward the land, can bring an animal. I try to remember to say thank you, to wear the same flannel shirt on each trip, to never be happy when the time comes to pull the trigger.

This may be sacrilege, but the spiritual connection I feel while hunting seems more authentic to me than Divine Liturgy on a Sunday morning. "This is the world Raven made," wrote Nelson, discussing the connection between traditional Koyukon people and their homeland. "Here, nature is not governed by God, as in Christian tradition. Nature *is* God."

Tundra seems to me more beautiful than New England leaves, if only because the high latitude makes sunshine itself feel like part of the changing season. After hiking for most of the day, I made my solitary camp near a raven rookery atop an outcropping of the Brooks Range, about a mile from the Sagavanirktok River, spackled with white excrement. The flock saw my approach from a half mile away, hovered above, circling. I recalled that a flock of ravens was called a kindness, and I interpreted the ravens' presence to mean I'd camped in a lucky spot. Later, I realized that I had it wrong—a roost of ravens is called an unkindness. In the long dusk of August, I listened to a female raven clack and click—*tsk, tsk, tsk*—like a scolding mother.

In the years since that first caribou trip, I've come to love watching ravens as they coast across the northern sky on their unscrupulous migrations. They are birds as filled with mystery as the landscape they inhabit, and I am always glad to see them when I hunt.

We see ravens as scavengers, but they contain the tenacity of the hunter as well. In spring, ravens sometimes gnaw out the eyes of newborn caribou as they drop from womb to frosted earth. They work in teams. One raven will distract the mother, squawk, land on her back or bite at an ear until, when the calf has been separated, another bird will pluck out the eyeballs. The calf wanders for days, bleating, searching for a place to suckle, and when at last it ends, the ravens descend upon the remains.

Such interactions rely on reciprocity, cooperation, and brutality but not meanness. The natural world doesn't include those kindnesses found in storybooks; the living world has nothing to prove. Back in their nests, the ravens will regurgitate food for their blue-eyed chicklets.

A friend on a climb in the Alaska Range once saw a raven circling above an icefall far up the Traleika Glacier, well beyond the alpine limit of animal habitation. Ten miles from anything alive, he had listened for an hour to the guttural screeches, the staccato shrieks. "I guess I learned we aren't the only species that goes to miserable places just for fun," he said.

Koyukon hunters say that when a raven rolls in the sky overhead, or "dumps their pack," you may have good luck on your hunt. Or perhaps Raven is just messing with you; after all, he can't really be trusted. Either way, the message is clear. The line between a successful harvest and a bad idea is, at best, a matter of luck.

Out beyond the five-mile road corridor, I set about preparing dinner and discovered I forgot fuel for the stove. The instant rice didn't rehydrate with cold water from my Nalgene bottle, and only after I poured my food into my bottle did I realize I had also forgotten my water filter. By the time breakfast came around, I was willing to eat the crunchy rice. To wash it down, I squeezed water from the moss and drank through a handkerchief to avoid the dirt. I was starting to feel pretty damn silly for having judged

Rick, Wayne, and Ryan's choice to drive around in a truck.

The nearby ravens lifted from the rocks and cawed. They seemed to be laughing at my ineptitude.

←——→

Here is the story I usually tell about the success of that first hunt: A small herd of caribou browsed the ridgeline at first light, and still in my sleeping bag, I glassed them with the rifle scope. I dressed quickly in the cold and crossed the spongy ground in silence. At the shore of a small lake, a cow offered me a long but clean shot. In that moment of quiet before my finger drew back the trigger, I hesitated. There is such finality to hunting. To kill an unsuspecting creature, no matter the reason, requires equal measures of courage and cruelty. She took a single step forward and dropped to the earth.

As I approached the kill site, my fingers made the sign of the cross—an instinctual reaction. Forehead, heart, Holy Spirit. I had killed and so I asked forgiveness; I had been given a gift and so I showed my gratitude in the way I knew how.

Later her calf appeared on a ridgeline. I had thought she was alone, but when I saw the milk seeping from her teats, I knew, and suddenly, I felt a deep and human remorse.

In the death of the cow, I had orphaned an animal. The ravens along the ridge waited. Perhaps they looked toward the calf's eyes. I could not bear the prospect of this animal's prolonged suffering. I did not want to leave the calf to wolves. I raised my rifle once again, and in a few seconds, it was finished.

←——→

I want so badly for that story to be the truest version of my first caribou hunt. But more than ten years have gone by, and now I am a father, and there is more I need to say. The clean shot I am so proud of went through her neck, and when I came up to her, she was still breathing, eyes wide, unable to stand, but a long way from dead. I stood there in a panic for a long time before I cut her throat.

It was legal to hunt cows then along the highway—you could take five animals of either sex—but I am not certain now that I made the right choice in killing the calf. I had wanted to prove I could hack it in Alaska, and that new-to-the-country naivety made it easy to convince myself I'd done the right thing. I worked hard not to question it.

And maybe it was okay. When we returned to Fairbanks, I hung the quarters in the cold space under my deck for several days to cure. A friend and I bolted an antique meat grinder to a cheap table. We cranked so hard for so long that that the table fell apart by the time we finished with the meat, and our shoulders throbbed for days. I threw a party at my dry cabin, and people brought even more meat. We drank beer around a campfire for two days and made so much sausage that the cased links encircled my house. I gave caribou brats to everyone I knew and gained fifteen pounds eating the bounty that winter.

Now, though, I am a father, and I still feel the lump in my throat at the inescapable, violent fact that once, years ago, I killed a mother and her offspring.

I dressed the carcasses alone. On moose hunts, only a fool will try to deal with fifteen hundred pounds of meat and guts by themselves. On most hunts since, I have been with someone. It is safer to have a partner in this remote country, but when you are with another, it is not the same. Together, you celebrate the success, comment over the amount of meat, and joke about how a camping trip has suddenly become hard work. Alone, I allowed myself to grieve, and to pray.

I sliced through the belly, delicately, until the stomach swelled, and her abdominal cavity emptied onto the lichen. My arms probed into her chest, tugged out the heart, lungs, spleen. The knife cut through viscous membrane until skin peeled away from muscle. Blood pooled along the spine, and I lifted the carcass to drain it onto the ground. Blood settled on my teeth, my arms, hands, and face.

When the task was done, I carried out the calf and the hide; the mother's meat I left to cool in the night. I drug the carcass a hundred yards from the kill site, a hopeful effort to dissuade scavengers. The entrails—intestines, stomach, the hooves and leg bones—I left to the ravens, already wheeling overhead. I had been two days alone on tundra, eating partially hydrated rice and drinking from the pools of melt that seeped through the rocks. It seemed good to give the gut pile to the land as tithe.

The next day, Ryan and the agents helped me retrieve the remaining meat. They laughed at me for my forgotten meals and tundra water but were happy to share in the labor of hauling meat. They hadn't been successful, and although they didn't say much about it, I had the sense that they were happy for a chance to walk out on the land.

We approached the kill through a patch of acidic crowberry. Ravens had cached the legs and nibbled at the guts, but the muscle meat remained untouched. Three birds rose from the intestines. I felt, even from afar, their ebony wings beating into the sky. I recalled how the previous morning they had circled me, performed acrobatics and announced my presence in the landscape. I had cursed the noise, birds warning me I had entered their territory. Yet when the caribou herd had risen off the lakeshore to the ridge, the ravens fell silent. They drifted into the upper atmosphere, waiting and watching, as if they knew it had become a hunt. Their sudden silence had almost unnerved me.

I had gutted the caribou, but I hadn't yet quartered it because I didn't know how. When a deer is killed in Wisconsin, all the hunters go out to the animal and admire it. They take pictures with the dead buck, crack open a couple beers. Then they drag it back to the cabin, camp, or barn with a rope and drive it into town to let the local butcher deal with it. So, I wasn't quite sure how to cut up 150 pounds of meat such that we could carry it on our backs across several miles of spongy ground.

Luckily, Rick talked me through processing the remainder of the cow. He demonstrated how to cut along the muscle fibers and how to saw through the pelvic bone. He helped me skin and roll the hide so it could get tanned back in Fairbanks. We worked together to load meat into our packs, with everyone taking a share of the load. The tension of those days driving in the truck dissipated. I felt humbled by Rick's patience in teaching me, and by everyone's willingness to work together.

We had different views and different goals, but I had begun to realize that the line between hobby and harvest was not as clear-cut as I thought. However noble I believed my approach to hunting to be, my connection to caribou and the tundra was tenuous at best. I just wanted something healthier, tastier, and closer to home than the graying beef from the Safeway cooler.

Not far from where we butchered the cow, we found a stash of antlers. We picked them up, felt their heft, held up the faded bone to our ears and posed for photos. I realized: these caribou had been making this migration for a thousand generations, probably more. Their stories, etched into a thousand meters of ancient frost piled upon the bedrock, could not be comprehended by human lifetimes. Everything about the caribou—the trails they walk, the rivers they ford, the lichen they paw from the snow in the winter dark, the splay of their hooves, the hollow fiber of their fur, the heat of their blood—bonds them to this land with a language as deep as the exposed limestone and shale bedrock in the cold hills where they abide.

The mysteries of a landscape only reveal themselves after years, decades, centuries. I have studied the animals I have killed, and I have tried to make use of as much of them as possible. I have eaten their muscles and organs, used their antlers for buttons on sweaters knit by my wife. The hide from that first caribou serves as a rug under the crib where my son sleeps. I have watched moose living across the seasons, and I have tried to always show them respect. I hope it is enough, but I do not know.

The wind picked up. It carried the beginning of winter. The trio of ravens descended to the caribou carcass again, hopped among the boulders, glared with black eyes. Their vocalizations were proud; they tore into the liver; one bird plucked a strand of sinew from another's back. Then—preening, yawning, gurgling— they rose into the Arctic sky.

We shouldered our loads of meat and trudged the six miles back to the road.

Learning to Read

S NOW TO OUR waists. Even with snowshoes, we punched
through the drifts along the edge of tree line. We slogged
through the crust for a mile, down into scattered spruce until a
boot path appeared where we entered the woods. We were about
twenty miles outside Fairbanks, and this was the eighth or ninth
time I had walked this trapline with my friend Ryan, a trapper
determined in his pursuit of winter fur.

We weren't expecting to get any animals, though there were
lynx and marten sets spread out across four miles of hillside here.
For the past week, the wind had blown hard on top of Mur-
phy Dome, and the weather in town had been warm. In interior
Alaska, warm means above zero, and when the temperature rises
above zero, it snows. Over a foot had fallen since Monday. We
had come out to clear the drifts off the traps, to keep the trail
open, to replenish the bait, and because Ryan was teaching me to
read tracks in the snow.

Tracking was what I most enjoyed about trapping fur. Animal tracks serve as teachers. They tell the daily life of a different
world, a world that, like an ethnographer, I wanted to study. If I
could understand the choices of a lynx or a fox, could gain insight

into their personalities, into lynx or fox society, then hopefully I could gain insight into myself, and into the human world as well.

A pair of tiny patter marks dashed out from beneath a half-buried and toppled spruce. A vole had recently skittered across the fresh snow in our trail, headed in a beeline for a stand of brush maybe four yards away. But midway, the tracks stopped. No prints doubled back, no hole burrowed down toward the moss. I knelt to examine the sign, and I could make out the perfect impression of beating wings, each strand of every feather brushed into the fresh fallen powder.

"An owl," said Ryan. I took a step, and in that move, the story, etched for a moment like carved crystal, disappeared, the owl and vole a lesson, a whisper in the winter sky.

←——————→

When I first started trapping, I tried to justify the barbarism, to portray trapping as a thing nobler than it is.

"The animals don't actually suffer that much," I told people.

"I try to use the entire animal," I said.

But then, in early December of my third season, I trapped my first lynx in a number four foothold trap. I had built a cubby—a tunnel of sticks against a tree that directs the animal to the bait—to lure the cat in, and my work had paid off. I came up the trail and found it already dead, a rare thing for a lynx. Usually they're alive, and to preserve the fur, you club their skull. Then, when the cat is stunned, you kneel on the chest and crush the life away. Sometimes you string a snare on a long pole, hook it around the neck, and pull tight until the lynx dies gasping for breath.

I'd caught my first lynx high on the hind leg. He had panicked, and in the struggle to escape tangled himself among the spruce boughs of the cubby. The drag—a log used to keep trapped animals from running off—lay tangled in a stand of alder. The cat had snapped his leg and bled out internally or maybe died of shock. He was frozen solid, his legs bundled underneath him as if still trying to run.

Animals caught in traps do suffer. It is a horrible thing to be tricked by the promise of food into a slow and suffering death. Still, death in the subarctic is never clean. Not when a gunshot takes a moose through the lungs, not when a wolf pack tears the guts from a caribou and leaves it to die, not when a duckling gets pulled under by a pike in the shallows of a stream, not when a mink sets off a conibear, a kill trap, and dies fast from a broken neck.

When the lynx died in my trap in that horrible way, I was overjoyed, pleased because I'd finally tricked a wild cat, and because there is nothing softer than the belly fur of a feline adapted to cold. Pressed against my neck, it seems the most lavish gift the boreal forest can provide.

This is not meat hunting, where a good shot and a few days' work will keep me in meat for the winter. I've eaten lynx, but only smothered in barbeque sauce to make it taste like chicken. I've eaten beaver roast, prepared with a recipe from a friend who grew up along the Yukon River. Mostly, though, I have used beaver meat as bait for other animals, who love its rank offal. Except for the fur, most parts of the animals killed trapping get thrown back into the forest.

I brought the dead lynx home, thawed it, skinned it. I stretched the fur and dried it near the heater in my cabin. I tried to forget about the way it had died, and when it was finally back from the tanner, I sat on the couch running my hands through the plush coat for over an hour.

←——→

The first time I saw a live animal in a trap, Ryan had me keep a .22 trained on the lynx, in case it pulled out of the foothold. It didn't. The animal sat calmly on the edge of the trail, looking at us with almost eerie circumspection. Ryan rigged a wire noose to a broken branch, looped it over the lynx's head, and in thirty seconds the cat twitched and died. It seemed clean, simple, as humane as it could be.

In my second winter in Alaska, I established a trapline of my own. I made sets along a steep slope not far off a snowmachine trail outside Fairbanks, and at first, I was proud. I made more than a dozen sets, and my line stretched for about three miles, looping down a ridge of birch trees where I found fox tracks.

Too many people used the trail. Once I came across friends who were letting their dogs run loose in the area. I pulled any set that could catch a dog immediately. I developed an almost pathological fear that I would catch someone's pet. When the snow deepened in late February, mushers turned up and sprung even my pole sets. I quit for the season, and the next year I found an area to trap that lay farther from town, where there was no trail and where no dogs traveled.

The only animal I caught that year was a marten. She'd tangled herself into a lynx cubby. I'd placed a small foothold trap deep in the cubby, in case an ermine crawled in through the back, and the marten's hind foot had been caught there. She was pissed, and not sitting calmly in the trail. When I approached, she snarled and flung her trap-caught paws at my face, bared fangs that suddenly looked enormous for such a small animal.

I emulated Ryan and rigged a noose, looped it over her head. I pulled tight. But she yanked at the noose with a bloody paw, stretched her body until every sinuous muscle torqued tight like a screw. She suffered for a long time. She gurgled deep in her throat, and at last I thought she was dead. I hung her carcass in a tree to retrieve after I'd finished checking the rest of my line. When I returned, she had revived, and though weak, had climbed to an alder branch, where she snarled at me and tore at the snare still around her neck.

I felt bad about that death, and the forest seemed to know I'd screwed up. For the rest of the season, I caught nothing.

It has always seemed to me that a good trapper has much in common with a good con artist. Furbearers are smart. A wolverine can smell steel. So can a wolf, and a poorly set trap that doesn't catch its quarry just teaches the animal to stay away. Around Fairbanks, where nearly every trail within twenty miles of town is strewn with snares and footholds, the fur populations are apt to be wary.

Trapping, then, is an act of prestidigitation, sleight of hand, trickery. And a good trick demands preparation. Trappers must learn to read the signs animals leave behind, because if we don't know the animals on our lines, mostly we're just hiking through the woods, building fantasy forts like when we were kids. Maybe, at the core of it, that is all trappers are doing anyway.

The more I learned the language of animal tracks, the more I was able to discern the stories. I learned to note where a spruce grouse flew because it smelled the stalking ermine just in time. I could find out whether marten were eating squirrels, hares, or grouse. Mostly in Alaska they avoid squirrels, and if they're in a heavily trapped area, they get wary faster, and won't often climb pole sets. I have seen where a fox climbed up on a stump to survey a wide swath of a forest fire burn. I have smelled the piss posts on the side of a trail where a fox marked its territory.

An otter in late winter will travel through the woods in search of open water. I've found their tracks glissading down a steep snowbank four miles from a creek. I have never trapped an otter. I have learned to discern a squirrel's winter food cache under five feet of snow by the tiny trails they blaze. In spring, a mat of chewed spruce cones extends for a dozen feet in all directions.

Learning to read sign helped me connect with the northern landscape. It provided mysteries to unravel. I didn't want to be a part of that world any more than a lynx wants to become a housecat, but different from the lynx, I longed to explore the edges of my civilized existence. When I pulled on my snowshoes or snapped into my skis each week, I imagined I was embarking on some great quest, and for those hours alone in the woods, I felt connected to a place where I didn't quite belong. I believed the attempt to skirt the hard and tenuous rim of a world more cruel than my own could help me make sense of my own humanity.

At the end of the day, I didn't always like what was out there. I'm not fit for that vicious landscape where a misstep into overflow could cost a foot, or a lazy finger around a beaver trap could take an arm, but, like fluency in a foreign language, trapping has helped me feel connected to something I don't quite understand.

I am not trying to justify my decision to trap. In my years of trapping, I caught six marten. I killed a couple mink, one or two ermine, and a lynx. I trapped a handful of young beaver. A few rabbits died in my snare sets. Mostly, I think I got lucky. I was never that careful about de-scenting my gloves or keeping fresh lure on the bait. A couple times, I made good sets but forgot to release to the safety hook on the conibear trap; when a fox came in to investigate, the trap sprung but didn't do anything except rattle about.

In recent years, I haven't trapped at all. The longer I have been in Alaska, the less important it seems to get out on the land to kill something. At least in part, I stopped trapping because I moved to a peninsula, where trapping pressure is higher and the animal populations more vulnerable. But that isn't the only reason. I look back at those first years in Fairbanks and wonder how much of my identity then stemmed from some inborn need to prove I could hack it in Alaska. I worry even about the way I learned to trap—a white guy teaching another white guy feels these days a bit too much like appropriation. I no longer feel like I need a specific reason to go into the woods in winter. I find plenty of joy these days just going for a ski with my family. Maybe the change has to do with becoming a father.

When I moved to the Kenai Peninsula, the musher whose dogs we were caring for taught me how to sew fur, and I felt relieved that my pelts could find actual purpose. I copied her patterns to make hats, gloves, and baby booties as gifts—and I made a few things for myself. I made Mollie a beaver fur hat for Christmas. I sewed my mother a pair of mink mittens. I made myself a marten hat and a thick pair of beaver mitts for winter bicycling. I don't wear the fur clothing I made for myself often; when I put it on, I feel uneasy about the image I must present. The fur feels so soft, so luxurious, that I can't believe I have earned the right to display such opulence.

←——→

I've met a couple of trappers who make their living by it, and it seems a hard life. They use airplanes or snowmachines to run fifty or a hundred miles of line in really remote places. They take in upward of a hundred lynx a year. They trap wolves and wolverine, animals where a single set can take more than a day to build, and the traps often produce nothing. It's a lonely life, one where you need cabins built at intervals along the trail, hovels that will save your life in the long winter, where if you don't plan well, you discover just how unpleasant mink can taste.

With wild animals, when the populations are well managed, furbearers rise and fall more because of the presence and absence of prey than they do because they are killed in traps. Still, I can't accept the old Alaskan argument about trapping bringing in good jobs and income for people. It's damn hard for a full-time trapper to break even, let alone make a living. And arguments about predator control mostly amount to political quackery; the policies reflect neither Indigenous ideology nor western biology. In the end, it seems to me that the only valid justifications for trapping must acknowledge the cruelty of it.

There are a number of stories among the Dena'ina about a boy who refuses to listen or learn. A 1975 recording of one of these "stupid boy stories," told by Nondalton resident Albert Wassilie, has the eponymous young boy going out with his mother and uncle to check a deadfall trap. When tripped, this traditional set releases a huge log, killing even a large animal almost instantly. The boy returns home and tells his uncle, "There's nothing in the trap. What should I do?"

His uncle tells him, "Just pull the bait." So the boy goes out, grabs the bait and, of course, gets killed. When his mother finds him the next day, she tosses the body aside.

"Your stupidity killed you," she says.

The moral? Life in the North is hard, so pay attention, think carefully before you act, and don't be stupid. It is as close to a reason to trap animals as any that I've found.

←——→

Trappers don't like to use visceral language about the killing. It's more comfortable to stick with terms used by politicians and biologists—to *harvest* or *take fur*. If we are successful in snaring something, we say a line is producing, not that we pinned an animal for three days by the leg and then strangled or beat it to death. Best not to linger on the killing.

None of the trappers I've met ever talked much about by-catch. Yet nearly every week, grey jays and red squirrels, attracted by a smear of beaver castor or the rabbit head wired to a tree as bait, ended up dead on my lines. I tossed them to the side of the trail because they made poor bait and had worthless hides. Once, I caught a boreal owl. It, too, I threw away.

This reticence to discuss the awfulness of trapping doesn't seem so different to me from other parts of human society. We hate to talk about the hard stuff. Though violence in our communities—both public and personal—is so common as to be inescapable, we prefer to use language that obscures it. When loved ones fall prey to drug addiction, abuse, harassment, alcoholism, or domestic assault, it's easier to say they're just having a hard time.

Once, when my brother called me to say that he found a dead homeless man in a park on his lunch break, I changed the subject. In the face of my own human failures with language, is it so strange that I don't want to talk about the animals I have tricked and killed?

For the most part, the dignified images of the wolf and the wildcat—the noble *National Geographic* portrayals—are coping mechanisms. When I killed that snarling marten whose leg had been mangled, I faced in a real way the prospect of a suffering death. Sometimes pain is unavoidable, and sometimes the worst pain comes because we are too curious about things better left alone.

I'm conflicted. More than once I have seen a fox loping across a frozen lake. I've watched lynx and otter fishing along stream banks, and I have been moved by their beauty. Yet I covet their skins because sometimes my motives are more hedonistic and gratuitous than they are respectful.

When Ryan taught me to case-skin a marten, to cut through the hind legs and peel the skin to the nose, he focused on taking care not to damage the pelt. Everything is about preserving the fur. Perhaps it is not such a stretch to imagine that this pursuit of fur might also be a way to preserve an essential connection, one we are at great risk of losing, with the natural world.

I see the act of trapping as a way to comprehend mystery. I struggle to grasp movements and motivations that lie beyond me. By the end of each season, the walk along my traplines would feel familiar, like a cherished book I could return to again and again.

In that way, trapping has something in common with reading. In both, we rely on clues to discern meaning. We build our expectations as the tension rises and get frustrated when the plot turns sour. At their best, both pursuits teach us that the desire to experience beauty can be fatal. Neither wilderness nor stories are apart from us; they're intrinsic to understanding ourselves.

Maybe I'm cruel, but the thing is, although I love the sensual feel of a soft fur in my hands, I loved trapping because out in the snow-frozen forests I discovered that life basically amounts to a rush of wings and a few footsteps. We fear the inevitable spring of steel jaws. We long to escape that moment when the coils release and snap tight. Most of us spend our lives striving to find some sense of comfort and safety and love, but in the end, often the only trace we leave behind is a breath of hollowed feathers on a drift of snow that will melt in the spring.

Remarks on a Jar of Squirrel

It is no wonder Moses, John the Baptist, and Jesus went into the wilderness to think. It is not just being alone. It's the smell of the air, the shapes of nature, the sounds—wind, birds, insects—the combination of being in a place where everything has a role—logical and explainable on one level—but is also a great enigma because the complexities and nuances of how it all fits together are beyond explanation and part of its wonderful mystery.

—DR. ALAN BORAAS, FIELD NOTES:
MYSTERY CREEK, ALASKA, JULY 3, 1986

*A*BOUT HALFWAY THROUGH December during my first winter in Fairbanks, a family of squirrels started to eat the insulation out of my roof.

The squirrels burrowed into my eaves. At three in the morning, they scampered above my head and scratched wood chips down onto my face. More than once I woke up with hives because chunks of fiberglass had found their way onto my sheets. Bits of batting littered the snow around my cabin like confetti. They chittered and chattered, and systematically replaced good pink insulation with a spruce cone cache.

Spruce cones, it turns out, do not make good insulation, and it gets cold in Fairbanks. Really cold. Mollie says the winters there can be hallucinatory. The only time I've ever been colder came during a season at the South Pole, and there are no squirrels at the South Pole. I had to do something—I was desperate. So I borrowed a crate of number one steel marten traps, baited my sets with a smear of peanut butter, and the bodies started to pile up.

I started getting more sleep. My heating bill stabilized. Still, something about killing those squirrels didn't feel right, and I couldn't bring myself to toss their bodies into a dumpster. Even though they were just squirrels, I imagined they might still have some worth. So, after I pried them from the traps, I let them freeze in a bucket on my porch. I told myself that before spring, I'd think of something.

In March, when the weather started to warm a bit, I asked around to see if anyone had ever eaten squirrel.

"Down South I have," said Ryan, who had loaned me the traps. "Up here, not even pine marten eat them. They probably taste like a spruce tree." He rolled his eyes and laughed.

I wasn't deterred. When a half dozen squirrels lay piled in the bucket, I brought them inside to thaw and started digging for recipes. In Irma Rombauer's *Joy of Cooking*, I found five methods for preparing squirrel. I called my grandfather, who grew up during the Depression in rural Missouri. He'd eaten squirrel, he said, but preferred opossum. Finally, in the University of Georgia Extension canning cookbook, I discovered a recipe for canned squirrel: "Soak meat one hour in brine made by dissolving one tablespoon salt per quart of water. Rinse. Use preparation procedures and processing times recommended for poultry, omitting the salt."

Alaska red squirrels are not the fat and fearless squirrels that inhabit university quads across the Lower 48. The squirrels in my roof were small, chipmunk size at best, with thick fur and muscles made for life at fifty below zero. It took me two hours to finish skinning and deboning, and when I finished, the quantity of meat wasn't enough to fill even a pint jar.

My plan was a bust. I tossed the scraps in a Ziploc bag, and they spent the next year getting freezer burned. Eventually, I did what I had tried so hard to avoid. I threw the meat away.

It has been over a decade since I arrived young and sure of myself and spent my first winter in Alaska. In those years, I've realized that interactions with this landscape come with a deep responsibility attached. I've learned that living close to the land entails more than just hunting, fishing, and planting a garden. And I've learned that killing squirrels, no matter what I tell myself, is not an act of reciprocity.

Not long ago, I participated in a local storytelling event and recounted my efforts to jar up those squirrels. I said my fight with roof-dwelling rodents helped me develop a connection to the North, taught me to reconceive what it means to live sustainably, and ultimately led me to call Alaska home. It felt good to tell that version of the story, but I'm not sure the interpretation is true. The more I think about it, the reason I tried canning squirrel meat had nothing to do with discovering a correct way to live; really, I just wanted to brag to my parents.

I grew up on a hobby farm in rural northwest Wisconsin. Twenty acres of swampy bottomland and the century-old buildings that came with it—house, barn, workshop, garage, and a motley collection of sheds—provided space to keep chickens, cut our own firewood, grow our own vegetables, and live close to the land.

We moved to the property when I was three, just before my younger brother was born, and my dad became a stay-at-home parent when we moved there. Instead of chasing an easily explainable career, Dad decided to put his energy into fixing up the farm. He has spent the last thirty-five years working on it, with no retirement in sight. My Mom retired a decade early from her job as a speech therapist to spend more time working on home improvement projects. For my parents, the property marks the endless pursuit of a lifelong dream.

As a kid, our family life revolved around building repairs, property maintenance, and the management of an enormous garden. Every spring, we planted potatoes, corn, cabbage, tomatoes, peppers, eggplants, lettuce, oregano—a running list of edible growth. We hoed and weeded and hilled all summer, and when time came to harvest, we filled hundreds of Mason jars with food for the winter months. My mother likes to recall that she spent most of her maternity leave after my brother was born "standing over the stove, stirring a pot."

We tapped maple trees every March to make syrup, an enormous labor that produced such a good dividend I still can't fathom regular table syrup. For several years, we went without a television—something that seems normal today but was unheard of among my elementary school classmates. We stripped the old farmhouse room by room and worked so hard on the renovations that I still sometimes taste sheetrock dust in my mouth.

The production of food and fixing of things were points of pride for our family, and major sources of conflict. I doubt they would see it this way, but something of my mother's years as a college cheerleader captain and my father's time in the navy seemed suffused in the perpetual repairs and digging in dirt. In the hoo-rah of dogmatic family labor, I came to view much of daily life as a series of chores. By the time I left behind the cornfields of rural Wisconsin for college, I thought of the house more as a source of stress than a labor of love.

My parents seem to enjoy maintaining their slice of midwestern paradise, even though it requires a nearly superhuman amount of upkeep. They're always busy transplanting fruit trees, gathering rocks for a new landscape project, canning, baking, cooking, mowing, plowing the driveway, performing incredible engineering feats to level the sagging barn. They collect new outbuildings the way Alaskans collect broken trucks in the driveway. Every few years, they add another building or repurpose an existing one; a family friend refers to the farm as "Messick-potamia."

And they hold themselves to incredible standards. The garden never has weeds. The hardwood floors get regular applications of fresh polish. The outbuildings are all painted the same barnyard red, and as best as I can tell, the windowsills get whitewashed annually. A few years ago, they restored the garden shed back into an outhouse, as it had been when they first moved in. They rebuilt it as a two-holer, with cedar paneling inside and a checkerboard between the seats.

If the work is hard, the result is a piece of property that feels like landscape art. Yet my parents' seasonal efforts often feel almost competitive, the jars in the cellar as much about the quantity produced as the quality of the nourishment, the kitchen floor as much about achieving aesthetic perfection as having a decent place to stand.

It has taken me a long time to question my parents' motivations for pursuing such a life, and even now, I feel uncertain about my position. It's a good way to live. My parents inspire their neighbors, share what they've made, and give huge parts of what they've reaped back to their church, community, and of course, to us in Alaska. I love them, and I'm grateful for the way they raised me. Still, for adult me, trying to square my younger identity with the realities of my life now feels a bit like dealing with that bucket of squirrels. I find a lot of well-intentioned ideas, but I can't quite figure out what parts still align with who—and where—I've come to be.

When I moved to Alaska, I found a landscape that exceeded every wilderness dream I'd ever had, but it still felt a lot like my parents' farm. The shabby cabins with their yards full of junk encouraged my most manic impulses. I could imagine a lifetime working on a piece of property here—only instead of fixing up an old homestead like my mom and dad, I could just build one from scratch. During the first years I lived in Alaska, I viewed the landscape the same way most people see it when they arrive here from somewhere else: as a frontier.

Frontiers offer the newcomer a hyperbolic experience—wild vistas, weird locals, an abiding sense of self-determination and freedom. A *frontier*, the word implies, is a place without history, where anything is possible and almost everything is permissible because nothing has yet become static. Here, living like a pioneer wasn't a choice that marked me as different from the neighbors, but a matter of survival.

My efforts to run a trapline, to fill the freezer with meat and berries, to take advantage of every available sliver of boreal forest bounty stemmed from the inborn belief that building connection requires hard work, and work gets judged by the quality of the finished product. In other words, to live a "real" Northern existence, I thought I had to do everything.

I pored over guidebooks and cookbooks to learn every useful plant, tree, herb, and berry north of the sixtieth parallel. By the time Mollie and I bought our house, gathering and growing good food bordered on a full-time job. Yet each passing summer, I felt more anxious, more stressed about how we could possibly do it all.

In the unrelenting labor of harvesting and preserving, the real value of living close to the land was getting lost. I never thought about why I wanted to gather food, only about how much more needed to be done. Amid the natural chaos of the northern landscape, I kept striving toward an impossible standard, with no time set aside to reflect on or even appreciate this life lived by the seasons. In other words, I wanted to live in Alaska the right way, but my way of doing it looked a lot more like obsession than connection.

Consider: In early April, I would pay attention to the birch trees. When the sap started to run, I'd think about the sorghum-like richness of syrup and tap a lot of trees, ignoring the lessons learned on my first job in the North, when I worked for a birch syrup maker who said trying to make syrup from birch sap amounted to insanity. Even with all the right equipment, they still worked themselves ragged. I had none of the right equipment, so I used a camp stove, burned sixty gallons of propane to keep the pot boiling, and gave up long before the sap sweetened to syrup.

When the first ferns poked up from the ground, I would fill a grocery bay with fiddleheads. Mollie and I hiked into the marshes to gather nettle leaves to dry for tea and make into pesto. We would pick buds from the cottonwood trees for muscle salve and search last summer's forest fires for morel mushrooms. At home, I'd spend a full day just cleaning the fiddleheads.

In June, wild roses, rhubarb, spruce tips. We would plant the garden and weed and weed and weed. In July and August, the berries ripen—haskap berries, strawberries, salmonberries, and blueberries, and I lived in pants stained purple at the knees and watched the windows grow mold from the steam billowing off the canner.

Every year, salmon pour into the rivers and you can catch them with a five-foot dipnet—wading out from shore with thousands of other Alaska residents—to fill the freezer with winter fillets. We have endured sleepless nights filleting, smoking, and canning. We have spent countless hours making salmon burgers, salmon soup, salmon spread, salmon jerky, and salmon roe caviar. I have smoked the bones and heads, simmered them, and strained the liquid for broth. One year we fermented the fish heads into a garden fertilizer so pungent that the smell knocked me to my knees from across the lawn.

I have spent hundreds of dollars in gas driving north for caribou, sat in the woods on rainy weekends in September calling for moose. A successful hunt means cutting and grinding, packing and wrapping. It means a half dozen trips to town for more freezer paper, calling friends for help to keep the meat from going bad.

We'd harvest potatoes, kale, cabbage, carrots, currants, peas. The slugs that attack the garden with the autumn rains required nightly vigilance to protect the brassicas. Even in late fall, the canner would hiss on the stove day and night, processing fish, meat, the harvest of low-bush and high-bush cranberries. There were always leaks to fix in the cabin walls; firewood to cut, split, and stack; and no matter how much is in the woodshed, it has never felt like enough.

I'd brew beer with the first snow and strap on skis to go look for the black growth of chaga on birch trees to grind into antioxidant powder. We would garble the dry herbs, spend hours plucking leaves from stems. I worked and worked and kept running the canner until the cabinets groaned under the weight of jams, jellies, teas, sauces, condiments, tinctures, vinegars, balms, soaps, oils, syrups, decoctions, infusions, cordials, wines, and elixirs. And in January, when the sun doesn't last long enough to warm the afternoon, Mollie would pull out the seed catalogs and place orders, and I would start to fret because spring was coming, and soon it would be time to do it all again.

What saved me from this manic cycle of labor and perfectionism came while renovating our bathroom. The original log structure of our home did not include running water; whoever added plumbing and the extra room to the house built everything wrong. They trapped moisture in areas that needed to breathe and ran leaky pipes through spaces that needed to stay dry. After two years, I decided we needed to at least make some mild repairs.

We both agreed that the work had to be finished by snowfall. So in August I peeled back the paneling on a corner with obvious dry rot and opened a Pandora's box. The boards in the foundation contained more ant colonies than wood, the walls were black with mold. The subfloor underneath the toilet was so decayed that we pulled it up in crumbling fistfuls.

One day in late September, with the project moving quickly toward serious marital crisis, our friend Alan Boraas stopped over. Alan had worked as an anthropologist at Kenai Peninsula College for nearly fifty years, and his insight into the history and lifeways of Alaska always left me awestruck. A quick question about the local Orthodox church would turn into a whole-day conversation. On visits to archaeological sites, he described villages, whose traces I couldn't tell from the muskeg, in ways that made the land feel imbued with sacred energy. Perhaps it was, and Alan simply channeled a reverential knowledge into all his work.

Alan mentored my teaching and opened my mind to more ethical, and honest, interpretations of history, religion, and the politics of place. Most of all, Alan was a friend whose kindness made us feel welcome in a new community. The previous winter, when he discovered we shoveled our driveway by hand, he started showing up after every snowfall—unless the Winnipeg Jets were playing—to plow us out.

I don't remember what brought Alan over that afternoon, but I remember the look on his face when he walked into a room with no floor or toilet, two entire sides of the house wrapped in blue tarps, and a roof held up with a couple car jacks.

"You know it'll be cold soon?" he said. I nodded and told him we were working on it.

I think back on that project and I imagine all the ways we could have avoided the horror of fixing everything ourselves. Paying someone else. Tearing it down. Moving. Instead, we did the demolition, the walls, windows, insulation, drywall, flooring, interior walls, new tub and toilet, washer, dryer, electrical, even the plumbing lines. We painted the siding and installed the tile in the bathroom. April came before we had a working indoor toilet. By the time we finished, I never wanted to do a home improvement project again. Five years later, even mild household repairs still fill me with existential dread.

At the time, I couldn't imagine another way. It was what I knew, what I'd learned, and I never thought to question the value of that peculiar kind of self-sufficiency.

When Alan saw the state of disrepair, he came over the next morning with his toolbelt and drill, and by the end of the day, we had exterior walls again. He never asked permission. He was over seventy and in declining health, but Alan had seen what I'd been too blind to notice, and too proud to ask for: to make it through winter, we needed help. He gave it without a second thought.

I did not know Alan nearly long enough. He died of a stroke in November 2019, a month before the birth of our son. In the months before he died, his son filmed an interview with him, in which he reflected on the work he'd done and the life he'd made in Alaska. "One of the principles in life," Alan said, "is you have to recognize important opportunities when they avail themselves. Because that's how you change the world."

For Alan, those opportunities included helping Indigenous communities fight back against the onslaught of a multibillion-dollar mining proposal. When a man named Peter Kalifornsky, the last living speaker of the Outer Inlet dialect of the Dena'ina language, approached him for help writing a book, Alan didn't hesitate. For the next four decades, he worked with Dena'ina leaders, culture bearers, and youth in the long process to revitalize their traditional language, knowledge, and worldviews, and he championed the value of that knowledge in the community. Just as Alan did with us, when people needed help, he was ready to get to work.

The longer I reflect on the way Alan showed up to help, without questioning, the more I think his behavior embodied real sustainability. His vision for a better North requires understanding the places we call home—whether chosen or inherited—not merely as slices of land, but as value systems, intricate connections, as whole communities.

Alan knew a new bathroom wouldn't help us create a utopian household. We just needed a place to pee. In a way, he showed me it was okay to let go of perfection, of idyllic aesthetics, and simply listen—to what people say, to what the land can tell us, and to what the history of a place can teach about how to live now. Listening, I think Alan would say, is some of our most important work.

←——————→

The choice to reorient my relationship with the land has required a kind of stillness that doesn't come naturally to me.

The traditional Dena'ina worldview, built around centuries of living on southcentral Alaska's lands and waters, holds that all plants and animals have a spirit. "Whatever is on earth is a person [has a spirit], they used to say," wrote Peter Kalifornsky in his book *K'tl'egh'I Sukdu: A Dena'ina Legacy*.

For the Dena'ina, the relationship between humans and the boreal landscape is so important that to pick even a blueberry becomes an act of ceremony. People must show respect in everything they do, because the nonhuman world is inextricable from the human one. In other words, knowledge about a place can be absorbed, and that knowledge moves in both directions. Plants, animals, stones, and fallen leaves are imbued with the knowledge of people who use them, and people are infused with the essence of those same items. The effort to make use of what we take from the land here isn't just about sustainability. It is also an act of reciprocity.

Alan described the Dena'ina spiritual connection in his work as "a unifying force—a social entanglement—that brings together members of a culture in a unique worldview and enriches their understanding of their place." Basically, he explained, if that knowledge is good, *beggesha*, it brings the good feelings associated with proper behavior. If it is bad, *beggesh*, the anger, violence, or misuse can be felt, and animals might leave, people could starve. How we treat the world changes everything.

For me, a white man, it seems easier to understand Indigenous ecology in terms of energy. According to the laws of physics, energy cannot be used—only transferred. All things, known and unknown, are contained in a kinetic movement from stardust to sea, from salmon to soil, from the blueberry bushes along the streambanks to the cobbler baking in my oven. The meaningful steps of existence branch outward, downward, to leaves and roots and connected sinews, shifting and expanding, taking on new roles and titles. Just as I am a writer and a father, a hunter, a gatherer, a meaning-maker, and a husband, so, too, does the rest of the world contain endless possibility.

Consider: When a moose eats a plant, and then I eat that moose, everything the moose has eaten becomes a part of me. If that moose has eaten well, then I get protein and rich flavor, and also aspirin from the willow bark, chlorophyll from the alder leaves, vitamin C from the tamarack shoots, rich amino acids from lake weeds. I become part willow, part moose, part swamp muck. If I eat a pig grown in a feedlot, I become part of the concrete and rubbish of the feedlot. If I eat a squirrel, I become part of the spruce trees whose cones were cached in my ceiling.

This is not simply about food. Even a house—like the log cabin where we live—takes on the essence of whatever those who live there imbue it with. If it is a good home, the home will feel good about it, and the tenants will experience grace. In other words, the good and bad—beggesha or beggesh—which we fill our lives with is as much a part of the land we live on as it is a part of us.

I am a guest in the North, an interloper, and my first inclination when I run up against one of life's endless challenges—sleepless children, broken plumbing, bad weather, squirrels in the eaves— is to root it out. As time has gone on, though, I've discovered the value of letting some things germinate. By studying the land, by listening to the wisdom of elders, and by learning to listen, I have started to rewrite my story. Like a mangrove seedling on the tide, driftlessness only ends when you bump against fertile soil. On the day we first saw the home where we now raise our children, Mollie and I sat together in the yard and felt the promise of family.

I am learning to weigh the labor of growing—which requires that we stay close to home—against the value of simply going out onto the land, nothing but full packs and time to wander the rivers and mountains. It often seems an impossible balance.

As time passes, we have discovered what we like and what we can handle. We no longer tap the birch trees every year, and when we do it is not so much to gather a product as to experience the change of the season as a literal flow, the liquid movement of a living world. I siphon the sap into a bottle and drink in long gulps.

Years of doting love alternating with seasons of benign neglect has transformed a weed patch into a garden and back again. The garden doesn't seem to mind the weeds and always offers an apothecary of northern herbs and berries that can sustain us year-round. Besides, our son enjoys picking dandelions more than he likes eating vegetables. When we have time, we harvest rhodiola root to help with our mood during the hard months. When we get busy, I remind myself that the rhodiola will be in the ground next year too. We pick berries and instead of jam, we mostly freeze them and drink smoothies. Except for an annual haul of salmon, the canner spends most of the summer in the cabinet.

The conscious acceptance of our daily reality has transformed harvesting from a chore to an opportunity to connect. In letting go of my obsessive need for accomplishment, I have a lot less to brag about to my parents, but I also find that I am much more attuned to the rhythms of the North. We no longer bother with tomatoes or cilantro. I'm happy to trade a jar or two of smoked salmon with friends in exchange for a little moose burger. Instead of expeditions to hunt and gather, we more often bundle up the kids and go for long walks or skis.

I've also realized that forging connection to place extends well beyond the harvest. Faith, too, plays a role in my journey. When I first started going to church again in graduate school, I remember feeling a deep sense of confusion around the service. I was listening to the same rites and hymns I'd grown up with, but the context felt foreign.

In my family, going to church provided a way to stay connected with an ethnic history severed by immigration. Mostly, holding on to cultural practices while detached from ancestral lands meant eating specific food—perohi on Christmas Eve, paskha, kulich, and kielbasa at Easter.

In Alaska I encountered a church history that was also a forced reinvention of Indigenous traditions, one that severed connections to the land without ever displacing the people. Ultimately, many Alaska Native people have found ways to retain some of their cultural practices within the context of this new religion, but the damages of colonization remain. I'm still working out what that legacy means for my own faith. My grandmother's recipes don't include much salmon, and on Sunday mornings, the fact that I grew up somewhere else makes me feel very conspicuous.

Sometimes I interpret my canned squirrel story as a metaphor for falling short—no matter how hard I try, I still can't quite fill the pint jar. I am not always the husband and father my family needs me to be. I rarely find that place where my writing feels both true to the story and to the vagaries of memory. I'm white, male, and still part of the problem. Despite everything, I am still an outsider.

But I keep trying, because foraging, gathering, and processing the boreal forest's myriad bounty teaches me to trust. I think the harvest can help me remember last summer, the fur hat can keep me warm, Sunday service can offer faith, writing can teach me to understand the multitudinous parts of myself, and the land can help me feel like I belong.

In some ways, my desire to understand Alaska has to do with atonement. Like most Americans, I was raised to believe in a society—the one that has shaped our nation and this continent— whose history, and present, is defined primarily by destruction. I am using borrowed knowledge and living on stolen land. For most of us, the essential connection between human knowledge and knowledge of the land we rely on was severed long ago, and healing that disconnect will likely require reparations.

It has become in vogue for progressive government and academic leaders in Alaska and elsewhere to acknowledge that the work they do is conducted on traditional Indigenous lands. At the start of meetings, a white person at the podium mangles a few words and makes a solemn, respectful statement before talking about the latest budget crisis.

This admission of a colonial legacy often feels, to me at least, disingenuous. Such statements, however well intentioned, don't really seek to change the paradigm. Obviously, it is a good thing for us to recognize the people who have lived here for untold generations and to be grateful for their stewardship. I'm not sure I can ever be grateful enough—this land nurtures my family. It sustains me.

Yet saying that we know we stole the land doesn't absolve us of oppression and theft. If we as outsiders actually want redemption, we need to shut our mouths, open our minds, and step back from ourselves. We need to put our hands in the earth, to eat fish and berries, to live by the seasons, and to listen to the original residents of this place, who have learned the land over millennia and know this place as medicine. Ultimately, if we really want those land acknowledgments to mean something, the answer seems obvious: give power to manage and maintain the land back to those we stole it from.

In 2018 I took a graduate research course on traditional ecological knowledge and wrote my term paper about the local Kenaitze tribe's effort to establish a "Dena'ina garden" for elders. The idea was to cultivate traditional wild plants in raised garden beds on the tribal campus so Elders could still practice harvesting. Traditional plant knowledge, then, wasn't just something that happened in the woods long ago but a living practice that could adapt to new contexts and modern realities.

For my paper, I interviewed Joel Isaak, a Dena'ina culture bearer and a friend, about Indigenous plant knowledge. The first thing he told me was that the value of wild food extends well beyond the dinner table. When you think about plants as part of an interconnected world, to harvest and eat them means you receive medicine, exercise, fresh air, and community.

The traditional Dena'ina practices that surround wild food harvests, said Isaak, serve as protection from dangerous psychological influence—isolation, disconnection, sequestration. In this way, gathering becomes ceremony, an all-encompassing experience that plays across seasons, decades, and millennia.

Getting our hands in the dirt is a gift, a heartline into the land, anchoring us to bedrock. Perhaps it is not so important how much we gather or how many jars we produce, but that we find ways to connect. In other words, the weeds in our gardens have as much value as the plants we cultivate, if only we are willing to accept the disorder. If only we are willing, the work of loving a place can also teach us the best ways to love ourselves.

←——→

A reciprocal interaction with the natural world changes what we value about a place, teaches us that the best way to sustain ourselves isn't through economy or product but by nurturing our relationship with the land. Like finishing the last stitch of a quilt and panning outward to discover a work of astonishing complexity, I believe that wild and local food can draw together communities, heal our ravages upon the land and its people, and offer us a path forward.

Of course, holistic interactions don't come easily. After all, I am seeking abundance in a land of scarcity. The North is a landscape of feast and famine, where the summer abundance gives way to a lean winter, and I often get it wrong.

I still feel the madness of the seasons, when everything is ripe and the rivers are full and I stay up late cutting fish, or when the darkness returns and malaise sets in and every moment of the shortened day feels like a wasted chance. When I am most stressed, instead of reaching out to the listening world, I turn inward. I think, if I can just get to the end, everything will be different. Sometimes I still compete with my parents. I brag that our berry bushes yield more than theirs. When they talk about their latest renovation, I spend the rest of the day feeling like I need to dust and polish the log walls. I still forget to breathe, to listen.

Often, before I go to bed in winter, I open the cupboard and marvel at the array of colors, at the beauty of food preserved in glass. The jars of smoked red salmon cascading into jams and jellies—raspberry, blueberry, rosehip, cranberry. Dandelion wine and spruce tip beer. Pickled things—fiddleheads, sauerkraut, and mustards. Mollie's tinctures, balms, and teas. Salves made from dried wild plants.

Before I became a parent, the cabinet, especially when it was full, gave me a sense of security. It offered proof of a job well done, evidence of the literal fruits of my labors. Since becoming a father, however, the cabinet has a lot less in it, and I've found myself engaging in a ritual I haven't even told Mollie about. I pick up an empty jar, hold it to my nose, and breathe deep.

Dena'ina gatherers say you should always leave an offering as recompense for what you have taken. Some burn sage, others sprinkle tobacco or leave strands of woven spruce root. For me, when I have finished gathering, I try to remember to cross myself and say a prayer. I do the same thing on Sunday mornings after communion, when I have taken the body and blood of Christ.

I hope my small efforts at ceremony make it clear how grateful I am to the land for what it has given, but I cannot be sure. The fact remains: there is no jar of squirrel on my cabinet shelves.

Bremner

Men go to the mountains to look out in amazement at the
huge waves of the sea and the broad flow of the rivers and
the tracts of the oceans and the stars in their courses, and
they overlook themselves.

—SAINT AUGUSTINE

THE IMMENSITY OF Alaska rarely dawns on me, but when
it does, usually I am in an airplane. Listening to the roar of
the propeller as we skimmed above rivers upon which no person
lived, into mountains graced with snow and silence, it occurred
to me that in remote places, such as the alpine valley where we
were headed, humility is essential. As the ground welled up
through the glaze of sky below our wings, I shuddered. The land,
I thought, teaches us to be alive and reminds us that we are small.

In December 2018 a friend contacted Mollie and me about
the possibility of volunteering the next summer at an abandoned
mining camp in the Chugach Mountains of Wrangell–St. Elias
National Park—the largest national park in the United States.
We leaped at the idea, talked ourselves to sleep with nameless
mountains and the idea of a writing retreat. We couldn't wait.

Then for four months we heard nothing, and life took a different course. We had been trying, and failing, to conceive a child for over a year. Mollie's cycle came and went, and in March, after nearly eighteen months of negative tests, we finally reached out to a doctor. I found myself at the hospital lab, where the receptionist directed me to the lobby bathroom with a collection cup and instructions on how to ensure a clean sperm sample. Mollie was poked, prodded, examined. When results came back, the doctor said getting pregnant wouldn't be easy. The word adoption slipped into the vocabulary of our evening conversations. I felt confused and angry because, as foreign as the idea of becoming parents seemed, the idea that we couldn't have a child at all seemed stranger still.

Finally, one morning in late March, the Park Service reappeared with a formal offer for us to spend the summer as caretakers of Bremner Historic Mining District. We accepted. Two weeks later, Mollie walked out of our bathroom with a positive pregnancy test in her hand.

After the doctor confirmed that we were indeed going to have a baby, after the tumult of joy and fear and uncertainty, we realized our plan to live for a season in a valley with notoriously bad weather, accessible only by bush plane, might not be such a great idea. Each morning Mollie woke up sick, we debated. We checked with our doctor.

"It's your decision," she said.

We told the Park Service about the pregnancy.

"We're okay with it if you are," they told us.

Perhaps, we reasoned, time in the wild would offer a place for Mollie to grow our child on fresh alpine water and air, where we could figure out how to become parents. Perhaps, I thought, if I could learn to listen at the pace of a mountain, I might wrap my mind around the mystery that had entered our lives.

We kept our plans. On the second day of July, with Mollie four months pregnant, we arrived at the gravel airstrip in McCarthy, loaded into a Cessna with the gear and food we would need for five weeks in the mountains, and took off.

A motley array of tin buildings spackled the green valley floor. Waterfalls cascaded from melting snowfields along the mountainsides. The plane wobbled in the wind, and I squeezed Mollie's hand. The tiny airstrip ended in a bluff, hemmed in by dense willows, and it seemed incredible that someone could land a plane in such a verdant and gusty place. We touched down without incident, unloaded our gear, and the pilot was off within minutes. He wouldn't fly us out until early August.

Our friend Kristin had come for a day to help haul food and gear up to the main camp, located along an overgrown road built by gold miners eighty-five years earlier. Two stream crossings soaked us to our thighs. Halfway up, Kristin spooked a bear.

It took two trips to haul everything to the dusty and clattering collection of buildings where we would live. While Mollie and Kristin relaxed in the alpine sun, I wandered about in a fever, agonizing over sleeping arrangements, moving things around, and running back and forth between the bunkhouse, the storage shed, the garage and workshop, the powerhouse, and the main office where we would ultimately decide to cook and sleep.

It felt as if the miners had just left, their belongings strewn through the buildings and rusting into the tussocks. My mind brimmed with questions. How had anyone, in the jumble of mountains and glacial outfall we had just flown over, found a way to get in here, or for that matter, a way to get out?

I would never fully wrap my mind around the seeming impossibility of all the stuff. That people spent six years blasting into bedrock and lugging thousands of tons of rock across this valley in a roar of heavy machinery seemed incongruous with the quiet and beauty of the wilderness. The tenacity they must have had, the skill, the lust for gold that made them nearly insane.

In the coming weeks, we would sift through the tin and spruce-board structures and find cans of butter, old shoes, picks, shovels, nails, lye, broken bedsprings, and ancient light bulbs. We would find mines hidden high up the slopes, nestled into inconceivable nooks on the shale cliffsides. We would trace old roadbeds as far as Monahan Creek, three miles up and over the valley, where an old woodcutter cabin rotted into the muskeg below tree line. We would sift through the broken remnants of vehicles, camps, a hydroelectric dam, and elevated tramways. Just as I had so many years ago, in that first Fairbanks dry cabin with the yard full of housewares, I wondered if we had signed up to live in a junk heap.

As the weeks passed, I learned to love the garbage we found as much as I loved the wildflowers. To understand a place, I realized, we must accept its history, the good and the bad alike. Sorting through the past can teach us to be mindful now, especially if, when we are away from civilization, we remember to pay close attention to ourselves.

Our first exploration of the area took us to the crest of the valley where the drainage split, dividing Golconda and Monahan Creeks. We looked down the meadow to a pair of small lakes maybe a mile distant, where the slope dropped steeply into alder thickets. Back toward the camp, water trickled through a scree field toward the tin buildings in the distance. The remnants of the roads still etched lines along the mountain's lower flanks, where they had once carried ore from the mines to a processing mill via a system of trams, pulleys, roadways, hydroelectric power, and makeshift contraptions.

Hiking up, we passed rusted cans, an overturned wheelbarrow, old tools, bales of cable, broken and unidentified mining parts. If we looked closely, we could discern the original runway.

The first runway had never been much more than some smoothed out tussocks. In 1937, a pilot flying in supplies to the mine caught the wheel of his plane in a pothole here and nosed his propeller into the thawing permafrost. The pilot had to clean the mud from his prop mechanism with a screwdriver, but he eventually flew out. The incident gained him the nickname Mudhole Smith, and he would be stuck with the name for the rest of his long and famous career as a bush pilot. The next year, the mine corporation applied for a government subsidy to put in a new strip farther down the valley. On the second effort, they used a bulldozer driven up in the winter months over the snow, and the airstrip remains today.

The known history of this valley is brief. After some mostly unsuccessful placer mining prior to World War I, a small consortium of enthusiastic miners scrounged up enough money to establish Bremner as one of the few hard rock mines in Alaska. They commenced mining in 1935 and ended in 1941.

The mine operated only in the summer months. In midspring, a couple of men flew in—or some years, drove machinery up the frozen rivers—to dig the buildings out of the snow. An average winter in this part of the Chugach Range can bring more than twenty feet of snowfall. The rest of the crew, which never numbered more than ten, arrived in late May, and they worked steadily until early October. Their only day off was the Fourth of July.

The labor and equipment required, coupled with the inaccessibility of the valley, makes the very existence of these mines staggering. Add that it ran on a shoestring budget using improvised machinery gutted from whatever they had on hand, and the venture to find gold in these hills seems nothing short of miraculous—and asinine.

We followed the meadow down through a dreamcoat of alpine wildflowers. Blue lupine and forget-me-not, yellow tundra rose, creamy saxifrage and cinquefoil, and pale pink valerian decorated the rocky earth. We found a pool of diamond-clear water tucked into in a glen that reminded me of Tolkien's Rivendell.

We stripped off our clothes, bathed. Mollie worried that the cold water might shock the baby. The simplicity of the day struck me—every hilltop view and bouldering nook felt like a stroke of luck.

In an alpine valley, the entire imperative of existence—to be born and grow and replicate and survive—must occur in the space of a two-month summer. A few clear days, and life thrives. The willows creep higher into the tundra. Fat and furry marmot pups tumble in the rocks. The cottongrass grows, spreads seeds, and gives structure to the tenuous soil. If it is cold and rainy, or if the snow melts late, as it so often does, then the plants must wait until the next year. The dirt sloughs off to bare rock. The animals starve.

So much of life resides on luck—a prayer for safe travels, good weather, the correct angle tunneling into a lode vein, a healthy child. After our swim, we sunned ourselves dry on the rocks and

I admired the swell of Mollie's belly. I wondered whether our child would be a boy or a girl—I hoped a girl. My mind dried on the wind and the moment blurred as I absorbed the warmth of gold-laced granite into my body. I felt like the luckiest man alive.

←——————→

We hiked up a side valley, past a broken tractor and the fallen platform that once served as the base for a cable tram, to the foot of a massive cirque. The route required a steep scramble along the edge of a waterfall and a jagged walk across a boulder field where broken tram cables wound through the rocks and nails jabbed up from rotting timbers strewn across the scree.

At the edge of a snowfield, I clambered up the steepening slope to a broad ledge that afforded a view of our route. I shouted down to Mollie that I found goat tracks and that the climb wasn't as bad as it looked. She began to climb and then, halfway up, she froze, glared at me, and turned back.

Later, we argued. I shouldn't have pushed her to climb such a dangerous route, she said. I protested. You're strong, fit, you've hiked up worse, I told her. But I'm pregnant, she said, and we're alone, and remote. Don't be stupid, John.

Suddenly, I felt ashamed, and for good reason. Bremner lay five hours by plane on a clear day from the nearest hospital, and even a twisted ankle would be a major injury out here. Mollie's decision to turn back was the one I should have made as well. I had been running around on the edges of cliffs, skipping along precipices, and exploring dangerous old mining relics. It was never about ability but about being responsible, about thinking like the parent I was soon to become.

The growth of a state of mind—the mind of a parent—still eluded me. That night, I lay awake and thought about how much our lives were being changed by the decision to have a child. I cataloged everything I could think of that a baby might need: crib, cradle, baby dresser, diapers, toys, clothes, boy names, girl names, a social security number. I wondered how many identities one person could hold inside themselves at the same time. Could I be a husband, father, lover, baby-bouncer, diaper-changer, adventurer, writer, and friend and still retain the capacity to see the world through fresh eyes? I suspected that all parents gave away great slabs of themselves the moment their first child arrived, and that the experience came as a rapture—part fear, part erasure, a full measure of joy.

The next morning, Mollie had a rare bout of second trimester morning sickness. After vomiting in the outhouse, she rinsed her mouth and said, "I know this sounds crazy, but I haven't felt this good in a long time."

In 1339 the Italian poet Francesco Petrarch wrote an account of a man climbing a mountain "because it was there." Though he was more famous for jumpstarting the Italian Renaissance and inventing the sonnet, it turns out Petrarch also gave birth to alpinism. Following his footsteps, I decided to make a solo circumnavigation of three valleys—climb over the cirque, into the next valley, and up Monahan Creek drainage back to the main camp. On the topographic map at least, it didn't look too bad.

I traversed upward, keeping a close eye on the weather and maintaining an angle of retreat. As I neared the saddle, maybe a hundred feet below the summit, I spotted a mountain goat nanny and her kid. I followed them through the rocks, hoping for a photograph, until they pranced up and over a ridge, and I looked down and realized that a bad step would send me two thousand feet to the boulders below. I looked to my right: not a hundred yards away, across a sandy scramble too steep to cross, was the entrance to Sheriff Mine, the canvas wall tent tattered but still intact.

Crazy-ass miners, I thought, and spent the next half hour picking my way back to safer ground, cursing my own stupidity. When I returned to my planned route, I found a snowfield cascading to the edge of a glacial cliff. There was nowhere to descend without crampons and a rope.

I took a few tentative steps out onto the snow. Below me, two creek drainages poured the nutrients of these peaks into the lowlands. The snow melting under my feet would channel and braid and fan down into the forest. Moose, bears, and salmon would traverse the banks, until finally, the water melting off this mountain would reach the sea. High enough to see the curve of the earth, I felt like I was experiencing the origin of water.

I only snapped out of my reverie when a pair of snow buntings landed beside me. I looked down again at the precipitous drop. Why had I climbed this high? Why had I considered descending the snowfield? I was about to become a father, for God's sake. I sat down on a rock to eat a snack.

In Petrarch's famous account, he fails to reach the summit. Exhausted and realizing he must turn back, the poet sits on a rock and writes: "when you consistently find yourself taking the wrong road in life, there comes a point when you either have to get up off your feet to try the path you've been putting off, or resign yourself to sinking even more deeply into despair."

I had sought this high peak because I believed it could provide adventure and maybe clarity. A few years earlier, I would have pressed on, but standing there, I knew what I needed to do, and it did not include a jagged climb down an ice chute. Perhaps it is best not to linger in places that cannot sustain us. I turned back.

"I'm going to be a father!" I whooped. Sand filled my boots as I glissaded a thousand feet down the talus toward more level ground, descending back to the ones I loved.

<---->

I was a fidgety child. I mean, really fidgety. Most of my teachers worried I had a hyperactivity disorder. My parents, desperate to find an outlet for my energy, enrolled me in every activity they could think of. I played soccer and Little League baseball, competed on the swim team, ran track and cross-country. I joined Boy Scouts, church groups, marching band, 4-H. I attended language camp, church camp, scout camp. And every summer from age eight until I was a teenager, I bicycled, first with my dad and later my mom, across the state of Minnesota on an organized ride for Multiple Sclerosis. I pedaled hundreds more miles to get ready for the event. When, as a new parent, I finally decided to get tested for ADHD, the positive result came as no surprise.

A couple weeks before Mollie and I arrived at Bremner, my mother flew up to visit. It was a mostly pleasant week. We hiked, cooked, spent time in the sun. But my mom is a former cheerleader, and she only has one speed. At age sixty-six, she still rocks air guitar solos—with her leg—on the dance floor at family weddings. I inherited my energy from her. During her few days with us, she sewed a blanket for the baby, weeded the garden, cooked, cleaned, played on her iPad, and talked continuously during every outing about life back home. Unless she was asleep, my mother never stopped moving and by the time she left, I was exhausted.

Ultimately, the fact that my parents engaged with my energy instead of stifling it helped make me a better person. Those childhood experiences shaped my curiosity, my desire to travel, my love for wild places. My mother's visit provided much-needed support and family connection.

Still, at Bremner I kept thinking about those childhood struggles because somehow, despite the lack of phone, email, and modern distractions, after a week in the valley I still felt overwhelmed by the busy life I'd left outside the mountains. My restless and frenetic energy kept bubbling over. I was still inventing meaningless to-do lists and unnecessary schedules, and I was annoying Mollie.

I started to think a lot about the coping mechanisms for my hyperactivity that I learned as a kid. If I couldn't sit still, the lessons of my childhood had implied, I should at least do something useful. By the time we had been at Bremner for two weeks, I'd hiked every gulley in a three-mile radius. I would pick an outcrop, a peak, a likely pass, and walk there. Increasingly, Mollie stayed behind to work on her knitting, and probably to get a little peace and quiet.

Hiking alone, those new overlooks failed to hold me in their sway. The constant exploration stopped being fun. And then one day I wondered: am I unable to sit still because I'm anxious and hyperactive, or am I anxious and hyperactive because I learned that stillness is bad?

That afternoon I had climbed beyond the old powerhouse and up to the alpine lake where the miners had built a hydroelectric dam. From there, I scrambled over a narrow pass and up another thousand feet to an unnamed summit. As I approached the top, the exposure took my breath away.

Above the thermocline, the air temperature dipped to near freezing. To the south, glaciers filled every valley. Clouds rolled off the snow, and a golden eagle floated upward on a thermal current directly in front of me.

Amid the clarity of the view wrinkled out before me, stillness came easily, but I wondered why I felt like I needed to work so hard to achieve it. I wanted to feel connected to land, to be bound to the beauty of this valley, but even on a mountaintop, I was still structuring my time and my energy with lists and things to do. I allowed myself rest only if I met my own arbitrary goals. For as long as I could remember, I had viewed relaxation as a reward. I realized suddenly that seeking stillness had never been about connection, and the rapture of the scene in front of me dissolved into petty worries and strange memories.

In junior high, when my already disorganized mind bellowed into puberty, my dad responded with militarism, modeled on his days in navy boot camp. I was supposed to chart my day into fifteen-minute increments, the activities cataloged in a faux-leather calendar. Walking the dog, doing the dishes, math homework, even casual reading was marked out on a timeline. If I deviated too far from the schedule, I faced long, abstract soliloquies about self-improvement techniques or my lack of consistency or the importance of follow-through. Those were difficult years; I fought with my parents a lot. When I left for college, I threw away nearly a dozen mostly empty day planners.

Twenty years later, despite the failure of those calendaring efforts, I was still using the same techniques to organize my life. Somehow, finding and sharing joy had become a task on a to-do list. Today I will go to the grocery store. Today I will weed the garden. Today I will climb this mountain in less than two hours, and I will return to the bottom in time to talk to Mollie for ten minutes and prepare dinner.

In trying to cope with my restlessness, I'd alienated the people I loved. I realized that no matter how efficient I was, if my life never veered from the to-do list, I would always fall short of happiness. I wanted to teach our child joy and hope, not fear and anxiety. I wanted to celebrate our child's energy, not harness it into something useful. I wondered: is this why gurus always lived on mountaintops?

When I arrived back at camp, Mollie was sitting in the meadow reading a book, looking very content.

"I'm sorry I'm such a mess," I told her.

She looked confused. I pressed my hands to her belly and sang song fragments into her belly button until she pushed me away.

A woman named Barbara Morford served as Bremner's caretaker for seventeen summers before we volunteered. She came from Wisconsin and approached her duties with gusto. Evidence of Barbara's efforts abounded, slipped in among the miner trash, trash which, after fifty years, was officially considered artifact. Barbara had made great progress in organizing the place. She had established an interpretive display, started a bunkhouse art project, and built up a store of camping supplies marked and labeled. They included spare chairs, spare cots, a three-year supply of toilet paper. The bunkhouse library, filled with books on Buddhism and self-awareness, came from her as well.

Three weeks into our tenure, we unearthed Barbara's logbook and found records of visitors, camp duties, and animals she had seen. The logbook tracked the number of cookies and brownies baked in a camp oven. It recorded her sightings of bears, birds, goats, and, once, a wolverine eating a marmot. It even noted the amount of cheese she had eaten, which at first seemed bizarre, but by week four, when our own supply had dwindled, it didn't seem such a bad idea to know how much cheese we ate.

At first the supplies and notes she left overwhelmed me. In my mind at least, I wanted things simple. Eat beans and rice, throw away the extra. Yet as we sifted through all the caretaker supplies, the search and rescue equipment, the emergency food, and the art supplies, I realized that for Barbara, Bremner functioned as a second home. As the weeks passed, I, too, came to understand this valley as home and to see our residency as an act of love.

I found a copy of Rene Daumal's *Mount Analogue* in the library. Part farcical climbing narrative, part surrealist experiment, Daumal's unfinished novel is as much a story of self-awareness as it is a quest. The book follows an expedition of spiritualist climbers up a hidden mountain peak, located on an unknown continent. Though Daumal died of tuberculosis before the novel was completed, the lessons contained in the existing chapters seemed a perfect analogy for our work at Bremner.

The climbing party in the novel spends months just to reach the base of Mount Analogue. On their arrival, the searchers discover that before they can climb farther, they must first learn how all parts of the great peak are connected. "The mountain is the bond between earth and sky. It is the way by which man can raise himself to the Divine and by which the Divine can reveal itself to man," writes Daumal.

Mountains lend themselves to such introspection. However simply we choose to live, our mark on the world follows us. Daumal says, "Even without wanting to, you always leave a few traces. Be ready to answer to your fellow men for the trail you leave behind." The summit, his characters learn, cannot be conquered; it exists as a state of the mind.

My desire for an uncomplicated existence at Bremner was earnest, but as time passed, I came to realize that the stuff left by Barbara—and by the miners—didn't indicate needless complexity.

It provided safety. When two hungry college boys hiked in on a multi-week mountain traverse, they were down to their last bites of food. We fed them, let them sleep inside. It was an easy thing for us. For them, it was lifesaving.

Perhaps parenting is not so different. From the valley floor, looking up at an avalanche chute, the climb seems impossible. All our preparations and planning seem suddenly absurd. The unseen dangers must be dealt with as we climb. Step by deliberate step, we move forward, noticing the changes in terrain and weather. We trust. We pray.

How possible such mindfulness felt amid the silence of the valley and the windy peaks. We even began to dream that the next summer we could return with our baby in tow.

We met the ground squirrels. Perhaps two dozen of them lived under the buildings throughout the compound. Chicken wire had been strung across the floors where they had scratched in looking for food during the decades of long winters. The bunkhouse visitor log seemed filled with anecdotes about how to combat their presence. Even old graffiti on the walls referenced the scourge of squirrels, but I thought they were too cute to be mad at. After all, this was their territory. I sometimes spent an hour or more just watching them gorge on grass seed in the meadows. In early July the squirrels were thin and wary; by August they had doubled in size, become fat and churlish, comfortable with our presence. We even gave one a name, Stuart.

We kept a list of bird sightings and learned their calls. Yellow warblers, golden-crowned sparrows, willow ptarmigan, palmated plover, Say's phoebe, wandering tattler, snow bunting, even harlequin ducks lived in the valley. We found nests in the tussock fields and in the rafters of the workshop. We listened to the songbirds chattering in the willows, along the creek, among the scree. We jumped when ptarmigan exploded from the brush, and we cooed when their baby chicks scuttled along the trail down to the airstrip.

At Bremner the snow melted in slow rivulets, the winds shifted each day, the birds, plants, and animals seemed born again each morning. We listened to rainfall and to the wind that rattled the tin shutters. We learned that the screams echoing across the valley came from marmots, and we kept an eye out for bears or eagles when we heard their bloodcurdling cries. In mid-July we went two weeks without hearing even the drone of a bush plane.

Mollie says that observing the world is the most important skill we possess. We experienced the valley across most of a season, and the slowness of it felt revelatory. I had nearly always traveled quickly through unfamiliar landscapes, and no matter the attention I paid, such interactions left me only a dominant impression of the people and terrain. The relative stillness of our time here was teaching me to see.

On our third night I stepped outside to pee at 2 a.m. In the deep dusk of the subarctic summer, I heard a rustling in the willows not twenty yards off. I shouted, and the dark silhouette of a grizzly bear emerged. I shouted. It jogged off toward the old workshop and disappeared like wind into the bushes. Surrounded by our food supply, the tin walls seemed suddenly far too flimsy. We slept poorly that night.

A few days later we saw the bear—a medium-sized bruin—again, meandering along the mountainside. About once or twice a week, he would return to the valley, now grubbing for roots, now chasing marmots, now eating berries—following the food of the season. One day I followed his tracks up and over a mountain pass, into the high scree among the peaks and snowfields, where there was no food, where the air was cold, the ground treacherous, where I never imagined a bear would go. Although we never walked without bear spray and we always warned the visitors about him, I came to think of the bear as a sort of neighbor. He didn't bother us, we stayed away from him—a good Alaska relationship.

Once we watched the bear trying to catch a ground squirrel on the hill above the old hydropower station. The squirrel had a safe retreat into a length of abandoned pipe, and for nearly an hour, we watched the bear dance around, trying to spook the squirrel into his mouth. He never succeeded, but we did enjoy the show.

We developed a routine. Each evening, we stuffed bear spray into a pocket and walked the old road down through the willows to the airstrip and back. By late July, the stream crossings had dried up enough that we could mostly avoid getting our feet wet. Each stroll revealed more of the land to us. A mother harlequin duck and her ducklings rode the rapids of Golconda Creek. An eagle hovering just a few feet in the air hunted marmots; the shadow of the bird's giant wingspan danced across the brush. We watched hopefully for ripening blueberries and caught glimpses of pika scurrying through the rocks.

The walks provided what my solo peak bagging could not—a way of being present with both the land and the woman I loved. I slept better. I worried less. I began to imagine myself as a father.

Mollie and I talked circles around the inevitable upheaval of our future. We tried to imagine our changing desires. We debated impending decisions. Should we quit our jobs? Should we sell our house? How should we parent together? Should we stay in

Alaska, and would we feel trapped if we remained here forever? As we learned to listen to the land, we began to listen to each other, and I think we both felt that we could lay claim to a new kind of faith.

Twice we took overnight journeys to explore more distant valleys. We justified these trips to the Park Service as "backcountry patrols." On the first, we hiked into the Monahan drainage and then up through a narrow gorge to the shore of an alpine lake. We camped at the foot of a waterfall, in a meadow blanketed with moss campion, and fell asleep to the sound of birds. In the morning, my birthday, Mollie made coffee and filled the tent with balloons. I tied them to my pack for the hike back to our main camp.

By the time we undertook our second overnight trek, Mollie barely fit into her clothes. She demanded huge amounts of snacks and took long naps when the afternoon sun warmed the tin walls of the bunkhouse. She now appeared visibly pregnant, and I was stunned by how alive she seemed. However, the hike, which entailed a traverse across a boulder field and fifteen hundred feet of climbing through willow thicket along precipitous rock slopes, left her exhausted.

I know this is obvious—men and women, Mars and Venus, etc.—but the life growing inside Mollie was a magical journey upon which I could not be invited. Adventuring together had formed the foundation of our marriage, but each day our realities grew farther apart. I could only marvel at the visible changes of Mollie's body, her breasts, hips, and belly swelling with new life.

Honestly, I wanted nothing more than to fast-forward to fatherhood, and Mollie's pregnancy made me feel like she was getting a head start on being a parent. Her journey seemed to me a kind of personal quest, one both painful and wonderful, toward self-realization and superhuman strength. And she made it look easy. In some ways, I was jealous

We eventually reached the alpine lake. The sun glowed golden over the peaks, and a storm swept off the icefields. A mother goat and her kid ambled five hundred feet above us. We crawled into our tent and listened to the rain sloughing rocks off the cliffside into the alpine pond.

I have loved living in Alaska, but after a decade here, I still don't feel comfortable calling it my home. Even at Bremner, where the beauty of the landscape made me an honored guest, I couldn't quite accept the fact that we were flown in to look after wreckage wrought by colonization.

Even as I find myself fascinated by the machinations of industrial efforts in this difficult place, I remain troubled by the history, politics, and economic drivers that reveal exploitation at its most raw and obvious. Industries—oil, gas, fishing, tourism, mining—work hard to promote a public narrative that justifies the destruction of the landscape and the historic lifeways tied to it.

They say: Nobody is using all this land; the animals don't mind. They justify: We love this beautiful state, and it shouldn't go to waste. They explain: Natives want industry, their corporations are leading the way, the world *needs* these resources. They shout: Drill baby, drill.

Age-old excuses, logical fallacies, bald-faced lies.

The truth is that Mollie and I were caretaking on land that already had stewards looking after it. Bremner valley lies along the mountainous rim of Ahtna territory, and Ahtna people have journeyed into the eastern Chugach Mountains to gather herbs and to hunt sheep or goats since time immemorial. Whether the Ahtna lived in this particular valley is ultimately irrelevant; the land here, regardless of what the deeds say, still belongs to them.

Here is the history as it has been written: First miners dug up the streams. Then the corporate gold and copper mines— Kennecott, Nabesna, Bremner, and others that pepper these mountain ranges—built railroads, runways, trams, entire company towns to pull out the ore. Then they left it all to rot. Homesteaders, big-game outfitters, and a handful of starry-eyed prospectors with more hope than sense moved in. In 1980 when the federal government informed people that Wrangell–St. Elias was becoming a national park, the white folks threw tantrums about it. Only recently have living Ahtna worldviews made their way into the narratives told about this area.

I spent several rainy days poring over the journals and archeological notes on Bremner. Neither the placer miners before World War I nor the lode mine operations during the Great Depression pulled enough gold to break even. Most years operations ran at a loss, and the miners spent winters begging for more financial backing in cities down south.

True, the innovation it took for the miners to get the gold out of here was incredible. The hydroelectric generator that pumped power from the dammed alpine lake, if hooked back up today, would likely still operate. Mineshafts were drilled and blasted into ridges that seem too steep for goats, let alone miners. Tram cars dangled over treacherous avalanche chutes to bring ore back down to the valley floor. The skeleton crew working here built buildings, stanchions, towers; milled their own lumber; drug up a Model-A dump truck on a sled one winter. They built several miles of roads, built and then rebuilt a runway. They operated a pilot mill that could pulverize up to fifty tons of rock per day.

An incredible operation. The archeology report by the Park Service highlights the effort here as an important part of Alaska history. It refers to "mining heritage" and notes that, "unlike the common portrayal of the Alaska miner either reaping bonanzas or suffering incredible hardship, the Bremner District helps to indicate that gold mining was also capable of yielding a working wage."

In 1940 the pilot mill processed 461 tons of broken rock into slag. Over the mine's entire operations, they pulled just $80,000 in gold from the valley—the weight equivalent of a couple gunny sacks full of flour. When operations ceased in 1941, the Yellow Band Gold Mine Company was almost $40,000 in debt. What a way to make a living.

Why do we delude ourselves and claim that landscapes devoid of people must be special—either preserved and pristine or forgotten and exploitable? Why do we insist that wild places must be inhuman, or that human achievements are always worth celebrating? What if the preserve-or-plunder binary has strained out the complexities of a real history, both human and natural?

Whatever we do to the Earth, we do also to ourselves, and to our descendants, for we are part of the planet's sway. When we silence the diverse voices that give meaning to a place, when we ignore the original lessons of the first human occupants of that place, when we focus only on an industrial history, or even a wilderness history, we create a narrative of Alaska that glorifies its own destruction.

I love Bremner for the way it brought me back to myself, but I cannot think of that valley without feeling at least some sense of collective regret. Across the state, more mining has failed than has produced. Those few who found gold usually left for warmer lands, and the artifacts they left behind include, along with leftover tins of food and piles of rusted machinery, mine tailings, polluted streams, denuded hillsides, and decimated animal populations. Should we really celebrate the detritus of their work?

A guided tour group from a fly-in lodge landed one day to look around. The guide showed them the powerhouse, the old truck, the bulldozers, offices, powerlines, the cast iron cooking stove in the bunkhouse. Apparently, the lodge had been bringing people to Bremner for decades. The lodge owner had come to Bremner as a boy, and the guide recounted a story about the last miner to live out here, in the late 1960s and early '70s, before the district was subsumed by the Park Service. The miner was a bit of a kook and, so the story went, he would drive a tiny motor scooter down to the airstrip to greet planes as they landed. When the pilot and passengers stepped out, he would zoom up on his little bike shouting, "I'm rich! I'm rich!" The scooter still sat in the shed, along with everything else.

The slow reclamation of Bremner by alder and willow gives me hope. In the failed industrial experiments that spackle the Alaska landscape, I see an apocalyptic vision that doesn't include nuclear war or zombies, but rather fireweed and ground squirrels.

Life learns to live among the failure we inevitably leave behind. Eventually, these tin buildings become for the squirrels what they once were for humans—habitat. Out of our greed something beautiful emerges, a more complicated place, a place more difficult to explain and understand, but a place worth leaving as a legacy for my child.

$\longleftrightarrow$

I believe volunteering at Bremner was the greatest gift we gave our child in the months before he was born. The mountains were a dreamland of wonders, inhospitable and embracing all at once.

The gratitude I feel now is not for the opportunity to explore wilderness or a history but for the time Mollie and I had to be wholly present with one another.

In Daumal's *Mount Analogue*, climbers seeking the summit are required to leave something of themselves behind before they can continue up the mountain. The idea is that those who come after them should not feel the loneliness and fear of being on a mountain alone. In the novel, this requirement creates a shared connection, a bond between people and land, tied together by community.

We were not hermits at Bremner, nor had we been wholly in isolation. Nearly two dozen people flew in to visit—day trippers in large groups, college boys on a wilderness trek, a family of four from Anchorage with a six-month-old. We enjoyed talking with the visitors, though we lacked Barbara's experience and brownies. We understood that our role as caretakers included fostering a community of people who also cared about this place.

The valley changed me. I was given lesson after lesson on how to live in the moment. When sunshine dappled the northern valley while thunder and lightning crashed off the glaciers to the south, or when the swirling morning fog lifted to reveal skims of July snow on top of the peaks, I felt myself opening to the natural rhythms of the place. Flowers bloomed, pollinated, and went to seed before my eyes. Ptarmigan chicks hatched, scuttled, and learned to fly. We shared the space under our bunkhouse with squirrels and marmots and watched them grow fat on seeds and grass.

At Bremner I learned the land a little better, and I learned how to better inhabit my own mind and body. I discovered that although we had created the life growing inside Mollie's body together and were now responsible for that life, we could not control the outcome of our child's existence any more than we could control the swirling of the mists across the ridgelines.

Bremner showed me a way into fatherhood. Our child grew from this valley, stretched out before us like the flow of a river. I had little to offer in return for such a bequest. I prayed.

When the time came for us to leave, we hauled our garbage and gear down to the airstrip. Though it was still early August, the leaves on the alders had begun to yellow. We had observed the valley across a full season. As we waited for the pilot to take us back to cheeseburgers, cell phones, and doctor appointments, I rested my head on Mollie's belly and felt the baby kick.

The baby did not come the way we imagined. On our return from the mountains, we learned the baby was a boy, and the news filled me with a sudden, irrational fear. How would we raise our boy to be a good man in this difficult world? In the doctor's office, I leaned into Mollie's belly and whispered to him—be kind.

We prepared a corner of our bedroom for a nursery. We installed a car seat, debated about diapers, clothes, and bottles. We picked out a name. The trees let go their leaves, and we took long walks through the woods. In the first week of December, although Mollie couldn't quite zip her jacket because of the baby, we went out skiing.

Then Mollie's blood pressure spiked. Doctor visits became daily events, a storm blew in, our car broke down, anxieties emerged, and the night Mollie went into labor, our boy defied the odds and turned breech. The next morning, after a failed attempt to manually turn him in the right direction, the doctor gave us twenty minutes to prepare for a caesarean.

Nurses strapped Mollie to a gurney, hooked her to beeping and buzzing machines, and shoved her through the operating room door. Someone handed me a pair of scrubs and sat me on a bench nearby. At a sink the doctor and nurses scrubbed their hands and chatted amiably, as if they didn't have a care in the world.

I felt sick. I wanted to scream. I simply couldn't wrap my mind around the suddenness of what was happening. We had lived in the mountains with this child. He was grown on fresh mountain air, on water made of nothing but sky and ice. We had prepared for everything, I thought, but not for this.

I started to shake. All the emotions I imagined I would feel in this moment, all my mountain dreams, were sliding away. My eyes went blurry, the room began to spin, and I slid sideways. Suddenly, the doctor was sitting beside me.

"I wish I could tell you this is the hardest part," she said, "but I can't. It isn't. Not by a long shot."

Far away Bremner lay underneath feet upon feet of snow. The marmots and squirrels were deep in hibernation. Silence and wind reigned among the high peaks, the winter darkness a blanket on the valley. I entered the operating room and sat down at Mollie's side, the doctor's words still ringing in my ears.

ACKNOWLEDGMENTS

*T*HIS BOOK WOULDN'T exist without the kindness, counsel, and support of an entire community.

At the top of the list is Mollie, my best friend, fellow explorer, and love of my life. Thank you for tolerating my numerous existential crises during the roller coaster of writing this book and for your courage, compassion, and your listening ear. Thank you for being my best and most ruthless editor, and for insisting I speak truth without losing beauty. Thank you for guiding us through our many journeys together, from swamp to river to nursery, and may our adventures never end.

Compass Lines first took shape during my time in graduate school at the University of Alaska Fairbanks. I have many people whose guidance through the MFA program gave me the perspectives that have kept me in the North. To my professors there, especially Daryl, Mary, Mike, Rich, David, and Alla, I am eternally grateful.

I have received a few awards that have supported my work as well. Thank you to the Rasmuson Foundation for awarding me the Individual Artist Award and to the Homer Council of the Arts, which gave my essay "Other Bloods" first prize in the 2021 Kenai Peninsula Writer's Contest.

Thank you to the friends whose careful reading and constructive criticism helped me believe in the manuscript and make this work shine, especially to Corinna Cook for her clear-as-glass comments.

A special thank-you and apologies to Jeremy Pataky, my publisher and editor at Porphyry Press. You've trusted my vision for this book, nurtured it into the best version of itself, and kept calm as I blew through nearly every deadline. Your vision for a northern press is worth believing in, and I'm proud my work can be part of that effort.

I also need to thank the huge number of friends and family whose stories and insights found their way into this work. To the friends with whom I traveled, especially Alex, Wade, Bassam, Ani, and Jim, thanks for putting up with me and for your wild spirits. To my early mentors Sean and Dave O, your belief in my work kept me going. I am grateful to my cousin, Father Ben, for pastoral advice and ecclesiastical knowledge. To Joel and Sondra, for your insights and kindnesses, I am indebted. Thank you to Ben Meyer for letting me include the plot of your novel as an excerpt—yours remains the best letter I've ever received. Thank you for babysitting our kids and for your never-ending array of wild ideas that nurture the inherent creativity and comedy of daily life. Finally, three mentors who supported this work are no longer here to share the joy of this culmination. To Alan, Bill, and Derick—I miss you, and I hope you can see the way your collective wisdom has shaped these pages.

Several essays in *Compass Lines* have been published previously, and I want to acknowledge the journals and magazines that have supported my work. A version of "Refrigerators at the End of the Road" first appeared online in *Cargo Literary*. The Alaska-based journal *Cirque* published "Learning to Read." *BioStories* published "The Fisherman and a .410 Shotgun" in both their online journal and in their *Encounters* anthology. "Desert Ghosts" appeared in *Rock & Sling* in 2015. Special thanks for that essay goes to Emily Hertz, whose work on the border did make a difference;

to Southwest Conservation Corps; and to my co-leaders Joe and Emily, whose tolerance of my wild younger self must have required the patience of a yogi. "Discovering Terra Incognita" was published in *Tampa Review* and selected as a winner of the 2013 AWP Intro Journals Prize. *Mud Season Review* published my essay "Throwing Stones at Apple Trees," which has been incorporated into the essay "Into the City of Jasmine" for this book. Another version of "Into the City of Jasmine" appeared online in *Nowhere* magazine, while snippets of "Remarks on a Jar of Squirrel" and "Of Big Burns and Ghost Towns" were published by *Superstition Review*.

No work is truly original, and the research that has gone into this book draws from a diverse wealth of sources. I have made every effort to cite specific sources as they appear in the text, and to confirm events, memories, or perspectives not my own with the owners of those ideas. Any errors are the product of my own mistakes or misinterpretations.

The epigraphs that open several essays come from works of literature I have loved, and for those who are interested, I share them here. The opening quotation in "A Clear Place in the Sky" is taken from Marjory Stoneman Douglas's book *The Everglades: River of Grass*. The lines woven through "Discovering Terra Incognita" come from a variety of sources, including Peter Matthiessen's *Ends of the Earth*, Apsley Cherry-Garrard's *Worst Journey in the World*, and Barry Lopez's essay "Informed by Indifference" in his collection *About this Life: Journeys on the Threshold of Memory*. The Heraclitus of Ephesus epigraph in "Big Burns and Ghost Towns" comes from John D'Agata's translation in his curated anthology *The Lost Origins of the Essay*. The title of "Learn the Flowers" is taken from a Gary Snyder poem, "For the Children," in his book *Turtle Island*. I first encountered this poem taped to Alan Boraas's office door. Alan held it up as a mantra for how we might think about ways to inhabit a given place. The epigraph for "Remarks on a Jar of Squirrel" was copied from handwritten field notes I found alongside sketches of archaeology sites in Alan's office while helping organize his papers after he passed away. Hopefully he does not mind the inclusion.

A final anecdote: In June 2006, I packed everything I thought I would need for a year in Korea into my backpack. My parents drove me to Minneapolis to see me off, and somewhere between the house and the airport, they discovered I didn't have any money. Not in my bank account, not in my wallet. They stopped at Emily's Lebanese deli, bought me a garlic pie to eat on the flight, and Dad slipped me forty bucks to get me through the first month abroad. I scoffed at my parents' worries then, and I still ignore most of the advice they give now. Despite such bad behavior, they continue to believe in my dreams. Their faith in my creative potential has been a guiding light, and I pray I can extend that same support to my own children. From the bottom of my heart, thank you.

ABOUT THE AUTHOR

PHOTO BY JEREMY PATAKY

*J*OHN MESSICK IS a writer, teacher, husband, and father. His work has appeared in news outlets and literary journals, including *Rock & Sling*, *Tampa Review*, *Nowhere Magazine*, *Miami Herald*, *Anchorage Daily News*, and more. John earned his MFA at the University of Alaska Fairbanks and was awarded an 2013 AWP Intro Journals Prize in nonfiction and a Rasmuson Foundation Individual Artist Award. He teaches composition at Kenai Peninsula College in Soldotna, Alaska, where he lives with his family. *Compass Lines* is his first book.